Management in a Liquid Modern World

Management in a Liquid Modern World

Zygmunt Bauman
Irena Bauman
Jerzy Kociatkiewicz
Monika Kostera

polity

First published in 2015 by Polity Press

Polity Press
65 Bridge Street
Cambridge CB2 1UR, UK

Polity Press
350 Main Street
Malden, MA 02148, USA

ISBN-13: 978-1-5095-0221-9
ISBN-13: 978-1-5095-0222-6 (pb)

A catalogue record for this book is available from the British Library.

Library of Congress Cataloging-in-Publication Data

Bauman, Zygmunt, 1925-
    Management in a liquid modern world / Zygmunt Bauman, Irena Bauman, Jerzy Kociatkiewicz, Monika Kostera.
        pages cm
    Includes bibliographical references and index.
    ISBN 978-1-5095-0221-9 (hardback) -- ISBN 978-1-5095-0222-6 (pbk.)
    1. Postmodernism--Social aspects. 2. Organizational sociology. 3. Social history--21st century. I. Title.
        HM449.B394 2015
        302.3'5--dc23

                                                        2015005697

Typeset in 11 on 14pt Sabon by
Servis Filmsetting Ltd, Stockport, Cheshire
Printed and bound in the UK by CPI Group (UK) Ltd, Croydon

Contents

Preface

Management has been most often applied to formal organizations such as businesses, governments, hospitals and so on. In these settings, management unsurprisingly carries connotations of control and organization ('Anna is responsible for managing 10,000 employees'). But management can also refer to coping or muddling through ('Carl managed to provide for his family in spite of losing his job'). Sometimes we manage others, sometimes ourselves; sometimes we manage to change things, sometimes to adjust to what we cannot change. Since most of life involves influence and adjustment, controlling and coping, changing and accepting what does not change, organization theory and management practice may be more broadly applicable than is generally recognized. The authors of *Management in a Liquid Modern World* will focus your attention on problems that characterize the biggest challenges we face in the world today – climate change, unsustainable levels of resource depletion, poverty, joblessness, and the natural, economic, political and

social disasters to which these conditions contribute –
and they will ask you to join them in imagining what
sort of management will help us to address and resolve
these problems. You will find many interesting ideas discussed here,
not least of which comes from structuring the book
as a series of conversations. The points of agreement
and disagreement that appear as Jerzy Kociatkiewicz,
Zygmunt Bauman, Irena Bauman and Monika Kostera
converse are both instructive and demonstrative. That
is, at the same time participants present their varied
views about the world's problems and options for solving them, they enact many of the ideas and suggestions
presented. Consider heterotopia as one example. The
participants discuss this idea as an alternative to both
utopia and dystopia, which have both been used to
seduce or shock people into changing how they live to
conform to an ethic that is represented in either positive
(utopian) or negative (dystopian) terms. Unlike both
utopia and dystopia, a heterotopia embraces not one but
many moralities and visions for the future and thereby
encourages acceptance of paradox, irony and contradiction, making them into common ground on which to
rebuild society in a pluralistic world. Intriguingly the
wide-ranging conversations this book presents offer an
example of heterotopia in action, showing how, when
effectively managed, different visions for the world
and the ethical and aesthetic values they imply can
lead to solidarity (i.e., a form of cooperation based on
accepting equality among humans rather than attempt-
ing to normalize their behaviour, which suppresses or
denies the differences by which they make their unique
valuable contributions to the whole).

The conversations begin with Zygmunt framing his approach to the world's problems with the idea of interregnum, 'a time-span of yet unknown length, stretching between a social setting which has run its course and another, as yet under-defined and most certainly underdetermined, which we expect or suspect will replace it.' Interregnum offers a chance to stop and consider possible futures, which might be the most desirable, and how to realize them. It also suggests one way of reading this book, that is as a momentary stopping point that will give you the opportunity to listen in on a conversation that can deepen your understanding of the world's problems and give you a change to act according to the ethics this book will also encourage you to craft out of concern for yourself and others.

Another powerful idea you will meet in this book is the growing need worldwide to trust the level of social organization that lies between constructing a massive global authority to control everything and everyone (often operating under the rubric of systems theory, which assumes that some small group is either smart enough or powerful enough to maintain this authority) and a conflict-generating individuality formed from self-serving choice. This in-between level is arising, our authors suggest, in organizations like cities – though cities, Zygmunt notes, are not 'conflict-trouble-and-worry-free zones . . . only . . . they are the sites providing relatively better – more realistic and promising – chances of confronting and tackling conflicts, troubles and worries pestering the present-day human condition at all levels of social integration'. Cities may not be the 'solutions', he argues, 'but [they offer] the best toolboxes available to produce them . . . they are means, not goals

– not the prospective destinations of the voyage, but the agencies capable of servicing the travellers'. Each participant in the conversation, in his or her own terms, pins hopes on this meso level, where management knowledge is most readily applicable, though managing management knowledge itself requires management. Lying between global institutions and self-serving individuals, in cities and small to medium-sized organizations, humans are better able to care for one another and thereby discover ways to cooperate to mutual advantage.

Pragmatism is discussed as one explanation for why cooperation at the meso level of the city can work where international-level efforts often fail. At the city level, one can experiment to discover what works and then adopt that solution *because* it works. By contrast, at the national or international level such pragmatic action is often frustrated by the inability to act and then learn from the outcomes of taking action. On such a large scale, mistakes are too costly, so learning based on experimentation is avoided, whereas cities and other meso-level organizations could be used as laboratories for experimentation. What this sensible position leaves out, however, is a view of how to manage the competitiveness that arises between meso-level assemblages of humanity. Returning us to the contradiction heterotopia embraces, Irena points out: 'It is likely that, as we discover the benefits of the city state, we will also come to remember why these did not survive as distinct units of management.'

I personally found it thought-provoking that three of the authors have resided for portions of their lives in Poland, a place where, having lived under the rule of Russian communism until 1989, many people are still relatively new to the effects of capitalist competition. This geographical and historical positioning allows Zygmunt, Jerzy and Monika to speak about revolution and solidarity as solutions to the problems of the world that might in Western contexts evoke suspicion, if not outright disbelief. Thus, when they decry and propose overthrowing the underlying assumptions of modern management, including competiveness as well as hierarchical structure and the ethos perpetuated by top-down control, I can almost see them reaching for what might be characterized in the West as an overly romanticized past. Yes, there certainly are things about cooperation, about self-management, about solidarity, about the crafted life that, as the authors maintain, are worth reintegrating into the driven lives we lead today – that is, if we are lucky enough to have a job, or motivated enough to work hard to make our living without the benefit of paid employment. And yes, some of the problems and possible solutions presented here can be usefully framed as having a moral imperative. I have few doubts that more cooperation and community, more caring for others as much as we care for ourselves, could help us produce better responses to the crises we face no matter which way we turn. But I also feel compelled to ask: isn't a search for solutions pointless in a world where, as the authors readily admit, no agreement on problem definition is likely (i.e., in the heterotopia)? Why not ask instead: what happens if we stop thinking in terms of problems and solutions? Problem/solution thinking is itself deeply embedded in the mainstream management consciousness they criticize as one of the many problems we face. As Einstein pointed out some time ago, we cannot solve our problems with the same kinds of thinking we used to create them. Analysing problems and mentally rehearsing alternative solutions, while an interesting occupation (that of the academic as much as the mainstream manager), continues the sort of thinking that got us into this mess in the first place.

So where do we go from here? The authors – somewhat ironically, given the downbeat character of their conversation at many points – offer hope as a good place from which to face the future as we emerge from the current interregnum. In the midst of clarifying and analysing problems of such enormity as those addressed here, hope might seem a bit too optimistic. Yet hope threads its way through the conversations in this book. Though clearly not a rational option, and possibly not sustainable, on a moment-by-moment basis hope renews us, raises our spirits, keeps us going in the face of what can seem insurmountable odds. What might we do if hope were sustained for however long we can manage it? Note that here I use the word 'manage' deliberately in the light of the book's major premise that management, at least in the ways it is newly defined by these conversations, offers us a reason to hope.

One pressing question remains: what should we hope *for*? The participants in these conversations offer several answers:

- Management without managers
- Cities as proving grounds in the search for *pragmatic* solutions to the world's ills
- A *new* socialist revolution based in the collective commons, heterotopia, sharing and collaboration
- Craftsmanship or making supported by Toffler's 'pro-sumers' who buy and sell on the Internet of Things

- Moving from sociality to cooperation and ultimately to solidarity.

While none of the items on the list is an altogether new idea, together they begin to suggest a vision of the world that breaks with what the authors decry as outmoded solutions. What else belongs on the list? As you read, I hope you will formulate your own contributions to these conversations and begin to take actions to realize them.

Mary Jo Hatch
Visiting Professor, IEDC Bled School of Management
(Slovenia) and Singapore Management University
(Singapore)

On interregnum, meso-level organizing and the city

Jerzy Kociatkiewicz I am really grateful to all three of you for agreeing to partake in this conversation-to-be, while at the same time giddy about the range of topics open for us to cover, as the task we are setting ourselves is by no means small, and we are unlikely to arrive at any definite answers in the course of this exchange. For while you, Zygmunt, have explored the consequences of your diagnosis of the current situation as liquid modernity for various and divergent aspects of our lives, the topic of management and organization in liquid modern times has remained relatively unexplored.

At the same time, your writings and ideas have served as an inspiration for, by now, generations of management scholars,[1] and you yourself have repeatedly touched upon issues of managing and organizing in your writings (perhaps most notably in *Work, Consumerism, and the New Poor*[2]); you have also lectured extensively in management and business schools. As yet, though, you have not collated these insights in a dedicated publication. This, then, is the task before us: to examine the need for and the possibility of managing in a liquid modern society, to investigate the continued viability of management ideas, and to explore the alternative viewpoints and seeds of change already around us.

You have written of the managerial revolution Mark II,[3] the process in which the managers are increasingly freed from the burdens of (but not the remuneration for) performing managerial duties, shifting the responsibility for the workers' performance onto the shoulders of the workers themselves. Self-assessment, peer-reviews and the general need to demonstrate one's own usefulness to one's superiors greatly streamline the processes of control.

In our own world of academia, researchers are now expected not only to be able to demonstrate the quality and the worth of their work (according to ever-changing but increasingly quantitative criteria – after all, comparison of quantitative data is much easier and less burdensome than the comparison of qualities irreducible to numbers) and to show the economic (again, hopefully quantitative) impact of their activities, but also to acquire the funds to pay for their research themselves without burdening their university with the unnecessary cost of their employment. And employment becomes an ever more elusive and temporary state. Universities – particularly, but by no means exclusively, American ones – are relying more and more on low-paid temporary staff who need continually to provide fresh rationale for their own employment.

Of course, universities serve here just as a convenient example, particularly striking because of the high educational requirements demanded of academic staff. The same processes can be seen in practically all other walks of life, where job security becomes an ever-more-distant, though still strongly coveted, prospect. The term 'precariat', popularized by Guy Standing[4] to describe the social class primarily defined by the precariousness of its work arrangements and social position, has gained widespread acceptance to the point of being included in a BBC-led survey study of the social classes of contemporary Britain (where it was claimed to comprise 15 per cent of the population).[5] All this seems like a bitter afterimage of the celebrated management scholar Charles Handy's[6] vision of the portfolio worker, unfettered by traditional organizational structures, accumulating experiences and knowledge, and working only on projects that seem particularly interesting or stimulating.

You have also argued that this arrangement is not a sustainable one and, indeed, calling on Antonio Gramsci's notion of interregnum,[7] you have described the current organizational and management regime as undergoing a profound crisis – if not an outright failure – of legitimization. There are indeed widespread signs of its continuing failure. The worldwide recession which is still very much with us was largely brought about by the banks' institutionalized irresponsibility[8] all over the globe. There are continuing (and ever more frequently publicized) cases of neglect and outright exploitation (which should be called criminal if not for the fact that perpetrators are still very rarely brought to account) of workers by Western companies' subcontractors, not just in the increasingly ironically sounding developing countries, but also in the more affluent areas including the European Union.[9] Last year, various beef and pork products sold in UK supermarkets were found to contain horsemeat. The subsequent investigation was remarkable not because of uncovered dishonesty and profiteering (we have come to expect these in any story of corporate misconduct), but because it laid bare just how little managerial oversight there is in the global economy of subcontractors.[10] It was not only the government investigators who were baffled and surprised by each new piece of evidence; the companies themselves (including both the supermarkets selling products and the so-called 'producers' whose logos appeared prominently on the packaging) turned out to be equally ignorant about the origin of their wares. In the much more tragic case of the collapse of Rana Plaza in Savar, Bangladesh, a building housing numerous textile factories, we could see the same patterns: companies fronting large, well-known Western clothing brands issued half-hearted denials of any involvement while scrambling for information about where in Bangladesh their recent batches of products had been manufactured. For all the 21st-century information technology at our disposal, clothing labels found in disaster sites turned out to be the most reliable signs of involvement.[11]

Interregnum, as its name suggests, is not just a time of collapse of the old order, but also the moment of possibility: new ideas deemed absurd within the old system can now be seriously considered, and new discourses can appear to try to make sense of what is happening around us. You, Monika, have devoted most of your research to finding new ways of understanding and managing organizations, and provide an essentially upbeat look at the world of possibilities before us in your latest book, *Occupy Management!*[12] You treat management scholarship and management education (in the UK alone, there were over 260,000 full-time students in management and administration programmes in 2011/2012, far more than in any other subject area[13]) as a crucial resource to be used for what might be termed the managerial revolution Mark III: the elimination of corporate structures of management and the actual empowerment of workers.

Yet the issue is not just one of the (re)distribution of power or agency: it is the much more important matter of the possibility of reconnecting work and morality. For Adam Smith, the great precursor of both economics and management studies, the two topics were inextricably bound and it seemed absurd to discuss one without reference to the other (as immoral or amoral models of economic development seemed to hold little interest or value). Yet, over the next two centuries, the two notions radically diverged to the point where business ethics exists as a separate topic and discipline with only limited crossover to other business and management subjects, and where a top-rated business ethics journal publishes articles defending sweatshop labour and violations of local labour laws by multinational corporations on ethical grounds of preserving (the easily dismissed) employees' free-market agency, and because the impossibility of devising uncontentious standards of fairness precludes discussion of exploitation in the division of profits between workers and multinationals.[14]

Thus, to buck the popular management textbook (and management course) tradition of including an ethics section somewhere at the very end of the book (or the lecture series), I propose that we start our discussion of organizations with the moral impulse (which, as Lévinas[15] forcefully reiterates, precedes all other relations or actions): where can we find it in the life of liquid modern organizations and their participants, what structures lead to its all-too-common suppression, and what chances are there for its acknowledgement and meaningful influence over the sphere of work?

Monika Kostera Let me just briefly interject a few words on the topic of the role of management in the time of interregnum – as you so accurately have depicted it, Jerzy, it is a phase lying between systems, in between working organizational and institutional orders, able to offer political, economic and cultural frames for human culture to function and develop in, and also to cultivate a sustainable relationship with the broader ecosystem. It is a liminal period, of unknown durability, characterized by fundamental uncertainty and many compelling questions, in place of what up till now has been regarded as the axiomatic truth, *ceteris paribus*, of modern economic faith. New working ideas of power and political settings, of markets – financial and human – and of the planetary consequences of ecological and social mismanagement are being urgently called for and the areas of problems caused by the lack of viable solutions are growing to ever more alarming proportions.[16]

The current system is perfectly unable, if perhaps not completely unwilling, to solve them; however, the only solutions proposed seem to be offered within the logic of a failing system – as Krzysztof Obłój so persuasively described it in mid-1980s Poland, *more of the same!*[17] Unable to offer new solutions, because that would demand a transcending of its limits, of its fundamental frames, it responds to all ills with well-trained yet completely unhelpful reactions: by invoking its axiomatic foundations and proposing solutions that 'should work' or 'are believed to have worked once'. If detailed planning is the problem, introduce more detail in the planning process! If centralization is the problem, more centralization! More formalization, more control, more limitations on trade, and so on.

Whereas the image intended by Obłój depicted another system, that of the centrally planned economy of what used to be called the Eastern Bloc, the mechanism of failing seems to be pretty much the same. More austerity, more tax privileges to the richest, fewer regulations on labour in the poorest countries, more outsourcing, etc. As in Krzysztof Obłój's brilliant analysis, then, the big picture seems to be just the same today: a system that has lost its ability to renew itself, to solve at least the problems it is itself causing, is bound to fall – is fallen already. However, if in the mid-1980s we, East Europeans, believed in the existence of a working alternative, another general way of doing things, a frame that would work for us as well as it seemed to be doing for the Others, the Western world – nowadays, there is no such easy and predictable template for change. What will come after the interregnum? We see no working example of something *instead* of what we, even in its failed current form, have today. I have no faith in science being able to predict the future – see what happened to futurology and sovietology – but I have propositions, suggestions concerning what can be done on a level of organizational practice – the meso level, in-between the broad, societal context and the micro-world of individuals and relationships.

This is what my book, *Occupy Management!*,[18] is about – how we can make a difference on the meso level by practices of self-management and self-organization, not waiting for the politicians or corporations to take initiative but by taking the initiative into our own hands. In the world of complete colonization of almost all human domains by management, in a world where virtually everyone has been educated in management in some form, at some point in their lives, we have all learned the basics of how to manage. I propose that it is time to use that knowledge to create meso structures – organizations – able to support themselves economically, which have different overarching aims from the current mainstream corporations and political institutions. The great Polish social activist and dissident, Jacek Kuroń, famously called out to the Polish society, then limited in its freedom of organizing by a dictatorship calling itself 'real socialism', not to burn (party) committees but to create ones of its own.

Interregnum, being a liminal phase, or a state betwixt and between more stable states and realities, was described by Victor Turner as a transitory stage, a state of blurred boundaries, where the usual constraints of normality and cultural definitions do not apply, where norms are relaxed and there is a special openness to experimentation and the creation of a sense of community.[19] During the liminal phase, strong and highly empowering bonds are created between people who go through it together, labelled 'communitas' by Turner. These bonds are based on humanity and much less defined by structures than are regular social and economic organizations. That is why I believe that the era of interregnum, which you, Jerzy, have described above – as bleak and unpromising as it may look – also has a strongly constructive potential. This is a time when we, the 99 per cent, by taking the initiative, self-organizing, can seek to make a real and lasting difference and work for a change on a much more global and systemic scale. By creating 'our own committees', we may, I believe, be building the premises of a new world, even if I am not sure what its more general rules, institutions and structures may be – not just waiting passively for the 'central committee' to fall. Passive waiting always frees space for other, more powerful forces to operate, rooted in the big nest of interests. What I propose in the book is, then, to start making a difference even before we know what the end result may become, or what the cause will ultimately be called: a form of self-management without a cause. What do you think of its prospects for accruing real critical mass, Zygmunt and Jerzy – in other words, do you think we can manage ourselves out of the crisis? Which brings us back to Jerzy's question about the moral impulse. Can the managerial revolution Mark III be based on the Lévinasian moral impulse on a meso level, where organizational relationships take place? What do you think, Zygmunt and Jerzy?

Zygmunt Bauman   You've set flying a genuine swarm of quandaries, issues, doubts, question marks . . . True, they are tightly bound together in a dense network of reciprocal and multi-focal dependencies, and once put into focus each one of them would be seen winking to all the others, yet all the same each calls for a separate scrutiny and a somewhat different treatment.

For instance, as Jerzy points out, 'Last year, various beef and pork products sold in UK supermarkets were found to contain horsemeat. The continuing investigation was remarkable not because of uncovered dishonesty and profiteering (we have come to expect these in any story of corporate misconduct), but because it laid bare just how little managerial oversight there is in the global economy of subcontractors.' By coincidence, a couple of days ago, BBC4 broadcast a *Hidden Killers*[20] documentary, revealing, among other half-forgotten worries of the past, like exploding toilets or spontaneously combusting clothes, that between 1831 and 1854 (that is, before health and safety legislation was imposed and a workable control system was started in earnest), adulteration had been found in Britain in 2,500 products 'from aluminum compounds in bread to lead chromate in mustard'. Almost two centuries later, the plague of food adulteration, allegedly done away with and buried once and for all by advanced modern management alongside many other pubescent but now bygone worries, seems to be rising from the grave. The question is, how did it happen? This is not a marginal question, judging by the massiveness of the resurrection; and the fact that, in a 'managed society', as with holograms or stem cells, every fragment reflects the totality, and from each one every other part of the whole can be extrapolated and regenerated.

Where, though, are we to start our search for an answer? Perhaps from what holds the contents of this reopened Pandora's Box together: the common cause, foundation and determinant of these and an infinite amount of other signals of apparent managerial laxity or failure? Jerzy finds an excellent candidate for such a starting point: the current separation and looming divorce between morality and the universe of work, production, distribution, trade we all inhabit. I would only add to that list the vast sphere of our personal interactions and exchanges, our way of 'being-in-the-world'.

Or, yet more to the point: our present-day mode of being-in-the-world – simultaneously together and apart. Jerzy refers to Lévinas,[21] for whom (as he rightly suggests) the moral impulse is not a *derivative* of society as has been all too often suggested, but rather the other way round: it is a *pre-social* phenomenon that 'precedes all other relations or actions'. Given, however, the *unconditionality* (one is allowed to say the *infinity*) of such moral responsibility for an-Other as that moral impulse inspires and demands, it transcends ordinary humans' ability to cope; as Lévinas admits, morality of 'absolute responsibility' is for saints – admittedly few-and-far-between occurrences if compared to the multitude of humans likely to find the volume of self-sacrifice merging on self-denial unbearable. More importantly yet, the 'moral impulse' in its pristine form, made up as it is to the measure of a 'moral party of two' and prompt to be released by the sight of the Other's face (any face, of any Other), is unfit to serve larger social groupings. Indeed, the very appearance of 'a third' renders the principle of un-conditionality and absoluteness of responsibility for the Other all but unfeasible and unsuitable for practical application. The presence of more than one 'Other' would inevitably raise quandaries that the moral impulse is unprepared to tackle. The well-being requirements of individual others may clash, be exceedingly difficult if not downright impossible to meet simultaneously; they can even be found to be mutually incompatible. Resources available to the moral person being as a rule finite, juxtaposing and comparing the needs of different 'Others' is called for – together with weighing their relative gravity and urgency as well as deciding which ones among them deserve to be awarded priority. But one of the defining traits of the moral impulse is its endemic blindness to differences between others, its inability to differentiate between their entitlements to care and making the care unconditional on the issue of entitlements.

No wonder that we find in Lévinas (though admittedly in a somewhat incompletely elaborated and implicit, rather than explicitly articulated form), a theory that explains the *raison d'être* of society and the functions which the society is called to perform in a way starkly different from Hobbes, who explained the indispensability of society by its task of preventing *bellum omnium contra omnes* (that scourge capable of making human life – as well as known to have made it – 'nasty, brutish and short') – the task of rendering plausible a peaceful coexistence of humans despite their being fatally endowed with inborn aggressive instincts. In the Lévinasian version, however, society is indispensable for almost exactly the opposite reason: society is needed to enable humans, burdened as they are – endowed or afflicted – with inborn moral impulses, to reconcile that burden with the harsh realities of shared existence, while salvaging what can be saved from the infinity of their moral responsibility. To perform that indispensable function, two instruments tend to be deployed.

The first instrument is the *codification* of moral obligations: cutting the infinity of moral responsibility implied according to Lévinas by its un-conditionality (as much as by the 'un-spoken-ness of ethical demand', as suggested by Knud Løgstrup,[22] another prominent philosopher of morality) – down to the admittedly limited, anything but 'infinite', performing capability of an average human. In Lévinas's terms, a finite number of conditions under which the – in principle, un-conditional – *moral responsibility* turns into a *moral obligation to act* are spelled out; or, to use Løgstrup's terminology, the messages of 'unspoken ethical demand' are unravelled, spelled out and recorded, again in finite numbers, which we can learn and follow.

The second is *adiaphorization* – exclusion of specific categories of human acts, or alternatively categories of their human objects, from the moral universe; rendering them ethically neutral, while subject to evaluation by other than good/evil criteria, allowed to supersede and ultimately make null and void the scores assigned to them on the scale of moral deeds. Just like the codification of moral obligations, adiaphorization aims at selective cancellation, or at least a temporary suspension, of moral responsibility – and serves thereby to prevent, or at least mitigate, the impact of such responsibility on probabilities of behavioural choices.

As the essential purpose of all and any management has always been and remains the manipulation of probabilities of human conduct (cutting some of them down, while enhancing some others), a regular deployment of both instruments is to be expected. And, indeed, both are commonly deployed in managerial practice – even if in varying time-bound and circumstance-bound proportions.

During most of the modern era, managerial strategies as recorded and articulated in Max Weber's ideal type of bureaucracy,[23] were focused on rendering the behaviour of subordinates maximally predetermined, and therefore all but fully predictable through eliminating or suppressing all and any factors of influence other than the commands issued by the superiors; as their major tenet, those strategies entailed the demand of suspension or even downright repression of personal idiosyncrasies (beliefs, predilections, affectations, mannerisms and eccentricities – as well as loyalties, commitments and obligations) of the subordinates for the duration of performing the tasks set by their superiors – that is, the reduction of criteria by which performance was measured and judged down to the single yardstick of 'the job having been done as commanded'. The side-effect of such strategies – not necessarily deliberately chosen, and time and again experienced as uncomfortably and irritatingly inconvenient – used to be the assumption by the managers of an undivided responsibility for the consequences of the command on the objects of commanded action. Released thereby from their responsibility *for* the results, their subordinates were in exchange burdened with the undivided responsibility *to* their superiors issuing the command.

The liquid phase of modernity brought in its wake a *sui generis* 'return of the depressed'. In the preceding 'solid' or 'hard' phase, the managers used to record individual idiosyncrasies of the managed on the side of *liabilities*. With a huge investment of mental and physical energy, financial expenditure and sheer ingenuity, managers tried (with only mixed success, to be sure) to repress those liabilities and, better still, to extirpate them altogether, as factors throwing out of balance routine and uniformity, the two pillars of an instrumentally rational performance and so also of a smooth and unswerving goal-pursuit. The same individual and personal, routine-resenting and uniformity-resisting singularities and peculiarities of the managed are now transferred onto the *assets* pages of accountancy books.

Rather than to be suffered and reluctantly endured as no less inescapable than undesirable facts of life, taxing and sapping the potential profitability of the enterprise, they are now welcome as ushering in vast and yet unexplored expanses of opportunity, and so an augury – and possibly a warrant – of unprecedented gains. The side-effect of that new managerial strategy is the shifting of responsibility *for the results* onto the shoulders of the *managed*, while reducing responsibility of the managers to employing them or laying them off according to the promise of profitability they hold for the enterprise – to the evaluation of their delivery, measured first and foremost in financial terms.

That seminal shift in the practice of management could not have been accomplished, nor would have been conceivably designed, were it not for the thorough deregulation of the labour market and conditions of employment and a retreat from the practice of collective bargaining and collectively negotiated salaries, wages and terms of employment: in other words, the thorough and well-nigh comprehensive *individualization* of the employer–employee relations. At least three of the side-effects of that underlying shift have been hugely consequential for the managers' position, role and strategy.

First, the task of managing situational uncertainty tends now to be shifted, to a fast-growing extent, to the managed.

Second, the managed are cast consequently in a setting that favours mutual competition and rivalry instead of solidarity.

Third, having been progressively reduced to the hire-and-fire decisions and released from the duty of continuous top-down surveillance and supervision, the bonds between the managers and the managed tend to be substantially weakened: a departure that conceals a massive growth in exploitation. Instead of purchasing specific skills and specified time from the managed, managers can now claim use of the totality of their time and all the – explicit or hidden, known or yet to be found and/or elicited – abilities and potentials of their employees, that radical expansion of managerial powers and entitlements being represented as 'increased autonomy' of the managed and 'flexibility' of their working times. The suspicion of a massively contrived *trompe d'oeil* has found a recent confirmation in the research report of Professor Cary Cooper of Lancaster University: it follows from his study that: 'around 40% of people are accessing emails on holiday – that's work . . . staff want to show that they are committed to try and keep their job in the next wave of redundancies'.[24] Cooper coined the terms 'presenteeism' (and 'electronic face time') for its email variety to denote that fast-spreading tendency for the 'flexibility of office time', which was intended to generate huge volumes of free – unpaid and unrecorded – overtime. Increasingly, that contrivance becomes an open secret – as shown, for instance openly, explicitly, without beating about the bush, by Marissa Mayer, the new boss of Yahoo!, in a message addressed to her employees: working from home is 'not what's right for Yahoo right now . . . Come into the office where we can see you, and look busy.'[25]

Knowing of such seminal departures in the substance of managerial activity and distribution of responsibilities, one shouldn't be surprised, dear Jerzy, let alone astonished, to learn 'how little managerial oversight there is in the global economy of subcontractors'. But where are we now, at the threshold of 2015? On the eve of another U-turn in the history of modern management? Calling retreat from a bridge too far, back to the old trusty ways and means of having things done through forcing other people to do them? Or are we rather facing the new managerial philosophy and practice rejecting the disguise it no longer needs: a disguise that has worked itself by now out of a job? Under the disguise of emancipation and new freedoms, we have been, after all, successfully re-drilled to be, 24 hours a day and 7 days a week, at the beck and call of our employers and reconciled to the effacement of the once gallantly defended boundary separating private time from office time – to an extent that doesn't allow the bluff of the scam to be safely called.

But allow me now to turn to Monika's searching questions, raising the big issue of a global agency capable of inducing global change.

Interregnum – the condition in which the old ways and means of getting things done have stopped working properly, yet the new, more effective ways and means are still at the design stage, or at best in the stage of experimentation – has its temporal (to wit, 'diachronic'), but also its spatial (that is – 'synchronic') dimension. Calling our present condition an 'interregnum', we refer to a time-span of yet unknown length, stretching between a social setting which has run its course and another, as yet under-defined and most certainly under-determined, which we expect or suspect will replace it. But we also refer to processes under way in the morphology of human togetherness, the structure of human cohabitation: old structures falling apart, their fragments entering new and untested arrangements, emergent settings spattered with blank spots and ill-fitting fragments in an advanced stage of disrepair, as well as with other zombie-like fragments, still mobile though out-of-joint and lacking obvious uses and applications – all in all, processes marking the condition of 'failing systems'. Incapacitated by the logic of 'more of the same', extant systems are, as Monika rightly concludes, 'perfectly unable' to face up to the challenge of de-, and particularly re-, composition. The structures that once interlocked into something reminiscent of a 'system' are now, clearly, in disarray. But the function of structures is to serve as catapults as well as a guiding/steering frame for action. In a state of disarray, they are, indeed, 'perfectly unable if perhaps not completely unwilling' to assure that this function is performed. Hence the big, perhaps the biggest question of the time of interregnum – fully and truly the 'meta-question', one that needs to be answered in order for all the rest of the questions to be properly articulated and for the search for answers to them to begin: 'Supposing that we know what needs to be done, who is going (i.e., able and willing at the same time) to do it?'

Wishing to pinpoint an agency capable of meeting the required standard, Monika – again rightly – focuses on the meso level of current social integration, having obviously, and once more rightly, disqualified both the uppermost level – the level of territorially sovereign nation-states – and the lowest level, that of the individual- or family-centred 'life politics', as serious, dedicated and reliable candidates for the job. I fully agree with her verdict. She is right on both counts – as territorial sovereignty, a relic of the 1648 Westphalian settlement signed in Münster and Osnabrück that has still, for the duration of the eras of nation-building and imperial colonialism, presumed to remain the universal precept on the world order, and has been practised as such, has by now, in the era of global interdependency, turned into an illusion; as to the postulated sovereignty of the individual, it had been an illusion from its birth – a figment of the imagination of governments keen to offload the protective obligations of the state. Though for different reasons, the actors operating at levels above and below the meso level of social integration are equally unfit for the job.

The 'meso level' stretching betwixt and between those extremes is, of course, a fairly vast territory, densely populated and encompassing a variegated multitude of formations. Not all of them are sufficiently promising to deserve having hopes for the resurrection of effective agency invested in them. At the moment, I am inclined to follow, however, the trail blazed by Benjamin Barber in his study/manifesto – as provocative as it sounds convincing – published in 2013 under the title *If Mayors Ruled the World: Dysfunctional Nations, Rising Cities*.[26]

'Today', states Barber: 'after a long history of regional success, the nation-state is failing us on the global scale. It was the perfect political recipe for the liberty and independence of autonomous peoples and nations. It is utterly unsuited to interdependence. The city, always the human habitat of first resort, has in today's globalizing world once again become democracy's best hope.'[27] Why are nation-states singularly unfit to tackle the challenges arising from the fact of our planet-wide interdependence? Because 'too inclined by their nature to rivalry and mutual exclusion', they appear 'quintessentially indisposed to cooperation and incapable of establishing global common goods'.[28] Why are the cities, especially the big cities, immensely more adapted to take the lead? Because of

> the unique urban potential for cooperation and egalitarianism unhindered by those obdurate forces of sovereignty and nationality, of ideology and inequality, that have historically hobbled and isolated nation-states inside fortresses celebrated as being 'independent' and 'autonomous'. Nor need the mayors tie their aspirations to cooperation to the siren song of a putative United Nations that will never be united because it is composed of rival nations whose essence lies in their sovereignty and independence.[29]

Far from being a utopian fantasy, all this is already happening, as Barber emphatically points out – even if unplanned, unsupervised and unmonitored. It happens spontaneously, as a natural phase in the development of cities as locations where 'creativity is unleashed, community solidified, and citizenship realized'.[30] Confronted daily by globally generated problems and the urge to resolve them, cities are already proving their ability to address the 'multiplying problems of an interdependent world' incomparably quicker and better than the ministerial offices of nation-states' capitals. To cut a long story short: 'Cities have little choice: to survive and flourish they must remain hospitable to pragmatism and problem solving, to cooperation and networking, to creativity and innovation.'[31] I believe all this chimes well with Monika's concerns. But I am eager to hear what all of you think of Barber's suggestions. And how do they square with your vision of the new and improved philosophy and practice of management?

JK   Thank you all for raising interesting issues which I hope we will be able to expand on in subsequent parts of our conversation: community and cooperation, morality and adiaphorization in the workplace, and the ideologies behind individualized relationships. At the moment, though, I think it would be wise to pause and reflect not only on Benjamin Barber's very intriguing book, but also on the wider ideas of cities as paragon organizations, or as signals of hope for democratic organizing in the times of rapidly vanishing legitimacy.

Cities are particularly alluring for organization and management theorists, for they represent the meso level in human endeavours, as suggested by Monika: poised between purely personal relations in families or small enterprises and the huge scale of global corporations or nation-states where complexity and diffusion of control obfuscates issues of management. As Lewis Mumford, the great theorist of urban space, observed already in 1937, the city

> in its complete sense, then, is a geographic plexus, an eco-
> nomic organization, an institutional process, a theater of
> social action, and an aesthetic symbol of collective unity.
> The city fosters art and is art; the city creates the theater
> and is the theater. It is in the city, the city as theater, that
> man's more purposive activities are focused, and work out,
> through conflicting and cooperating personalities, events,
> groups, into more significant culminations.[32]

As such, the city appears to be an ideal setting not just for its inhabitants to shape their surroundings collectively, but also for the researcher to observe and analyse managerial processes in their fullness – including contradictions and paradoxes, as well as harmonies and grand strategies. Barbara Czarniawska's studies of big city management (in Rome, Stockholm and Warsaw)[33] are perhaps the best exemplars of research focused on understanding cities as organizations: complex, full of conflict and divergent ideals (as well as of neglect and incompetence), but able to contribute to the common good of their disparate participants.

Yet Barber's claim is much stronger than just to present cities as significant organizations, or as vital links in the constitution of a contemporary social order: he presents them as the most hopeful means of building a sustainable, democratic economy and of working towards our common wellbeing. This seems to me a continuation and development of a very old, and compelling, view of urban living: already the medieval Germans proclaimed that 'Stadtluft macht frei' ('urban air makes you free' – possibly implicating cities in the dismantling of the feudal social order), though we could reach farther still, tracing the origins of Athenian democracy to the rise of the city-state.

Thus, the very notion of a city is intimately tied to the idea of governance, of the linkage between power and politics that you, Zygmunt, have identified as undergoing (or, indeed, having undergone) a messy divorce in the course of globalization.[34] City infrastructure (both physical and institutional) brings together place, human experience and the ability to self-organize that are the prerequisites of successful political action.

Yet this is the moment where I hesitate, perhaps just because of the complexity of urban conditions, and the multitude of different symptoms, problems and solutions that cities present to us. Writing about cities some ten years ago, you, Zygmunt, have identified the twin forces of mixophobia, manifesting itself in 'the drive towards islands of similarity and sameness and amidst the sea of variety and difference',[35] and mixophilia, the desire to seek out and befriend strangers, to celebrate diversity, to embrace idiosyncrasy. You saw hope for the cities of the future in the possibility of adjusting the balance of this antinomy, of strengthening mixophilia even as we accept that mixophobia will forever remain an indelible part of human experience.

Monika and I, studying urban spaces a few years later, were struck by the ubiquitous attempts, undertaken at various levels of municipal management, to sanitize the experiences of passers-by and inhabitants – attempts, that is, to excise all negative emotions and their manifestations (such manifestations including the poor, distressed, or unhappy people) from publicly accessible urban environments.[36] The perfectly contented city is, of course, a rather mixophobic notion, relying as it does on the Other ceasing to appear as the whole human being possessed of a wide range of feelings and emotions (and, probably, denying such negative emotions in oneself as well).

But here lies what I see as the biggest problem of the city as the paragon organization of the future: its relation with inequality, poverty and deprivation is a complex and difficult one. The World Health Organization reports that, since a few years ago, for the first time in the history of humankind, more than half of the planet's population lives in cities.[37] At the same time, another United Nations agency estimates that one third of the global population inhabits slums,[38] putting a question mark over the claim that cities benefit all their inhabitants (even if not equally). Mark Davis eloquently summed up the problem in the title of his excellent book chronicling the indignities of modern city sprawls, calling our urbanized world the *Planet of Slums*.[39] Edward Glaeser, an unabashed enthusiast of urbanization, argues it is all a problem of perception: cities do not produce poverty; they attract poor people precisely because urban settings offer pathways to a better life. Poverty is just as abhorrent and deadly in rural settings as it is in the city, though it might be less visible and offers less hope for improvement.[40] In most places, indeed, life expectancy is higher in urban areas, but there is little to suggest eradication of poverty or greater equality is coming as a result of urbanization. And Barber's excitement about cities as the model of progressive management is tinged with much more caution and unease – I do not mean to imply he is unaware of the darker side of urban development, of crime, corruption, and power abuses inherent (or at least prevalent) in municipal social patterns and structures of governance; he notes that 'With the challenges of inequality so embedded in the political and economic infrastructure and their origin at least in part associated with national and global forces outside and beyond the control of the city, remediation is extraordinarily difficult. Only with innovation and imagination is inequality likely to be touched.'[41] And while I think we can all agree with the call for imaginative and innovative ways of reworking organizations that are still dominant, if no longer trusted, in our times of interregnum, I remain hesitant about whether cities represent the best candidates for such an endeavour. The dark image before my eyes is that of the continued unaccountability of the entire global network of financial markets, comfortably anchored (or perhaps nested) in the municipal stock exchanges (be they in New York, Tokyo, London or Hong Kong), whose undoubted influence over host cities is not balanced by any reciprocal regulatory power of the local powers-that-be (or of grassroots protest movements such as Occupy Wall Street, demanding tighter oversight of global corporate entities). Considering the devastation wrought by the financial crash of 2008, this is a serious issue that requires truly imaginative and innovative solutions.

ZB You are, of course, right when you observe that modern cities are anything but medium-sized models of the big-sized ideal society ('ideal' in the republican, not in the currently common, indeed well-nigh 'common-sensical', liberal, or the vulgarized neo-liberal, sense – to take a leaf from George Orwell, 'ideal' in the sense of 'decent society', that is a society struggling to combine liberty and equality with fraternity[42]). You are also right when you point out that all the woes and malaise that haunt present-day big societies can be found inside the city – and in an even more striking and off-putting form, more salient and discomforting for being condensed and cramped within a strolling or jogging distance, and so that much more palpable, tangible and obtrusive than those encrypted in national statistical tables. But neither I nor Barber[43] (if I read him correctly) suggest that cities are conflict-trouble-and-worry-free zones. We only imply that they are the sites providing relatively better – more realistic and promising – chances of confronting and tackling conflicts, troubles and worries pestering the present-day human condition at all levels of social integration. To put it in a nutshell: the 'really existing cities' are not solutions, but the best toolboxes available to produce them. More importantly yet: they are means, not goals – not the prospective destinations of the voyage, but the agencies capable of servicing the travellers.

Take mixophobia, for instance: it is conceived and born in, and sprouts from, the motley crowds congesting city streets, but it also emanates from disconcertingly illegible and confusing mental maps of the world, concocted as they tend to be of disparate and uncoordinated bits and pieces of second- or third-hand knowledge. In the first case, however, the victims/carriers of mixophobia are close to the sources of the problem and so it is in their power, at least in principle, to examine them, as well as design, test and deploy effective remedies: an eventuality hardly conceivable in the second case, in which the enormity of distance from the sources, far transcending the testing skills, equipment and powers of mixophobia's victims/carriers, renders it all but impassable.

Cities are sites where thought and senses meet; they meet, so to speak, bodily – in flesh and bones – not just in the mental callisthenics of a sage or dreams of a dreamer. Some – perhaps many – of their encounters may prove to be what Martin Buber[44] dubbed *Vergegnungen* ('mis-meetings', wasting the opportunity for dialogical engagement) rather than *Begegnungen* ('genuine meetings', steering on both sides from the 'I–it' towards an 'I–thou' posture). But, in urban life, thoughts and senses can't avoid frequently repeated encounters (just walking a short stretch of a city street offers them in profusion) and so the chance for a *Begegnung* is immensely greater than in the hours spent online, in 'interaction' with a digital source of information – when the user has the option of locking herself or himself in a tightly sealed 'echo chamber' or 'hall of mirrors', options totally absent in living subject to the urban-life logic. How wise it was of you, Jerzy, to recall the long-lasting, time-immune conviction that 'Stadtluft macht frei'. When it comes to being free, rather than fixed and immobilized, the sheer breathing of urban air releases you from the torments inextricable from choosing freedom over security. In the city, freedom is not a matter of choice – it is a fate. Freedom is one condition you are *not* free to surrender, however strongly you may desire the cosiness of a voluntary servitude, and however hard you may try to follow your desire. And freedom, as I hope you'd agree, is an alloy of endless opportunity with an endless risk. It is for that reason that cities are the natural habitats of creativity.

But freedom has many faces. To everyone wishing to grasp their unique traits and the differences between them, I recommend Quentin Skinner's lectures, published in 1998 under the title *Liberty before Liberalism*.[45] Skinner presents there the as-unwholesome-as-they-are-common practices in which Hegel's urge of *catching the time in thought*[46] comes into its own. He points out that the scholarly practitioners of such catchments are all too often 'bewitched' into believing that the mainstream way of thinking 'must be *the* way of thinking'. Skinner is, and rightly so, nonplussed. He insists:

> The history of philosophy, and perhaps especially of moral, social and political philosophy, is there to prevent us from

becoming too readily bewitched. The intellectual historian can help us to appreciate how far the values embodied in our present way of life, and our present way of thinking about those values, reflect a series of choices made at different times between different possible worlds.[47]

This is needed – insists Skinner, referring to Lewis Namier – to stop political theories acting 'as the merest *ex post facto* rationalizations of political behaviour'.[48] After all, 'Hobbes's Leviathan is no less an artifact of seventeenth-century culture than Purcell's operas or *Paradise Lost*.'[49]

A major point in Skinner's story is that we have all been 'bewitched' by the 'liberal' idea of liberty, but the present-day liberals of the Bentham/Berlin/Hayek/Freedman/Reagan/Thatcher congregation, far from being the inventors of the modern idea of freedom, have twisted it beyond recognition and invested it with a thoroughly different social/political/cultural meaning. The cause of liberty was pursued quite a while before its presently dominant 'liberal' (for the sake of clarity, call it '*neo*-liberal') version prevailed. That presently dominant version reduces the issue of liberty to its 'negative' side: denial and elimination of all and any constraints imposed on choices following each individual's conception of her/his interests. Not so, however, the 'neo-Roman' theory that precedes Jeremy Bentham and his heirs by two or three centuries and which Quentin Skinner draws, for our benefit, out of oblivion, where Isaiah Berlin's eulogy of 'negative freedom', coupled with ridicule and dismissal of its positive complement, had cast it: 'The neo-Roman writers fully accept that the extent of your freedom as a citizen should be measured by the extent to which you are or are not constrained from acting at will in the pursuit of your chosen ends.' However,

> what the neo-Roman writers repudiate *avant la lettre* is the key assumption of classical liberalism to the effect that force and the coercive threat of it constitute the only forms of constraint that interfere with individual liberty. The neo-Roman writers insist, by contrast, that to live in a condition of dependence is in itself a source and a form of constraint.[50]

If, as I do, you agree with Skinner's rather than Berlin's theory of freedom, then we need to consider together how it affects the substance of the on-going U-turn in managerial philosophy and practice. Does it, indeed, as we are made to believe, serve the expansion of individual freedom? Does the deregulation of the labour market offer the sellers of labour expansion of their freedom? Does the 'flexibilization' of the terms of employment offer employees more liberty than the now-abandoned stiff routines of supervised work? All in all: does the shift of responsibility from the managers' onto the subordinates' shoulders liberate the latter from obnoxious managerial interference, leaving more to their own discretion? Or does all that allegedly 'emancipatory' drive amount to nothing more than shifting the emphasis from direct application of force or threats of coercion to a permanent and unassailable condition of dependence – while leaving the chances of genuine, fully fledged freedom of choice as few and far between as before? Given the evasive, diffuse, blurred and 'capillary', rather than focused (and therefore salient, tangible and easy to locate) nature of constraints arising from dependence, can't this shift make freedom of choice yet more difficult to obtain, defend and retain than before? It is, in short – and resorting to distinctions introduced by Harvard Professor Joseph S. Nye[51] – replacing in the arsenal of domination the costly, awkward-in-use and increasingly unpopular weapons of 'hard' power with their 'soft' variety, hardly less oppressive and overwhelming, only more attuned to the present-day cultural idiom. And doing it not so much for the sake of greater autonomy and liberty of the objects of domination, as in order to make the domination yet more comprehensive – while rendering resistance to it more difficult, and so an effective resistance much less likely than before.

Left face-to-face with ambient uncertainty, its challenges, dangers, risks and costs, as well as the full responsibility for failing to cope, have the objects of new-style management become freer than they were under the old regime? This question calls for close scrutiny – and by the results of that scrutiny the social, political and moral values of the present departures need to be measured and judged.

2

Management without managers?

Monika Kostera Going back to Zygmunt's question concerning possible guiding frames for action, I'd like to invite Irena to join the three of us in a conversation about the future. Hoping for ideas from all of the interlocutors, but aiming my question firstly at Irena, I would like to reflect upon the proposition that we should now, somehow, seek ways to manage ourselves out of the current crisis we, as humanity, have found ourselves in. In particular, I am interested in the idea of managing beyond the managerial elite, the possibility of revolutionary management.

The three of us who begun the conversation agree that the present times can be regarded as a period in-between working systems, an interregnum. The laws of economics, principles of management, models of organizing seem to have ceased working, or at least ceased to bring the results they once did – that is, by creating an appearance of cause-and-effect relationships. There is no enthusiasm to be found or commitment to spare; only twenty or thirty years ago, business leaders like Lee

Iaccocca and consultants like Tom Peters were able to unify people and get their trust, commitment and faith in the organizational ideas they stood for and proposed. Nowadays, nobody much seems to be really enthusiastic about businesses and organizations; people concentrate on their private lives, think primarily of their families and the future of their own children and engage less in public matters. Politicians are more and more often despised; in most countries, people withhold their trust completely from the public sphere and increasingly from the organizational sphere. A kind of social tunnel vision develops when few care about making a difference and even fewer wish to change the world for the better. Yet the current system, while not working properly, seems to be at least drifting forwards, and, as a colleague of mine, an anthropologist, remarked, there does not seem to be a way out of this; the world is simply going to the dogs and everyone is complying. Or, as one of my young students said, nobody likes it but what the hell can we do about it? Both the researcher and the student agreed that the world should become, once again, a place to live, a place where there is hope and where people and the planet are more important than the interests of anonymous investment funds and financial indicators. And I have the impression that most people I talk with share this conviction, while many share the anthropologist's and the student's fatalism. Earlier, Zygmunt cited the 'big meta-question': '"Supposing that we know what needs to be done, who is going (i.e., able and willing at the same time) to do it?"'

Indeed, that is the big question, and I would like to learn your opinion, Irena, about possible agencies of change, but, going back even further, to the common assumption in our initial conversation regarding the state of the world, do you agree that what we are now experiencing is a systemic and managerial void, a state of non-management, an interregnum? Another – issue, that is – for me, connected with the idea of interregnum, is the notion of adiaphorization. As Zygmunt explained earlier, the current era is characterized by the excluding of events, experiences and social actors from the moral categories. I believe that management has become one of these excluded domains, to which general ethical codes, or even human conscience, do not seem to apply. They have been replaced by a construct called 'business ethics' that refers to ethical standards and moral choices in business that are generally distinct from other spheres of life. Yet the practice of morality in work organizations seems to be not only unmoved by the discussions undertaken in journals of business ethics but largely unchanging since at least the seminal work by Robert Jackall,[1] who, based on his fieldwork carried out in the mid-1980s, portrayed the activities of corporate managers as engaging in the creation of an elitist in-culture, thereby limiting the scope of input based on criteria such as conscience and moral consideration. Their actual rules and standards were based on the opinions and norms of that group, resembling the chit-chat of a social club much more than the ethos of a professional or moral community.

In liquid modernity, this social club and its moral practices have become adiaphorized, and now, in the interregnum, its actions are excluded from the moral fabric of social life, and at the same time its actions are ceasing to have a real impact, because of the incapacity of the system. This is creating a strange and rather un-splendid state of isolation for the managerial caste in our contemporary times – the hitherto ruling class suddenly bracketed out as if disconnected from the rest of the social sphere, becoming more of a spectacle than a vigorous collective social actor, not unlike the British aristocracy before and just after World War II. My second question to Irena and then all of you, my dear interlocutors, concerns the managerial revolution Mark III. Returning to my earlier query, we have already discussed the potentials of the meso level for holding new structures and forms. But the question remains: can this revolution be based on compassion and on the Lévinasian moral impulse enacted on the meso level? My current wrangling with this question concerns Jerzy's initial definition of this revolution as such. Do you agree that it needs to bring about the elimination of corporate structures of management and the actual empowerment of workers? And if so, who are the next managers if not, perhaps, the managerial social club as it is now? Do you agree with me that the managers of the old era are becoming slowly but certainly disconnected from society? In other words, are we to witness and perhaps participate in management without managers?

Irena Bauman Thank you all for making space for another voice within your conversations.

In accepting your invitation, I know that my voice is that of a practising architect and of an urbanist, and, as such, will be different from yours. However, the direction of travel will remain the same. I am offering, as Zygmunt often offers himself, to enter the same room (this conversation) but through a different door.

Management without managers?

Before I can engage with Monika's challenging questions, I need to step back into your initial conversation and define two significant differences between our respective points of entry.

The first is that I would like us to include environmental crisis in our thinking, in addition to those already identified by Jerzy – a crisis that, unlike those others, presents an existential threat to all humanity, and will, therefore, be an increasingly significant catalyst for innovations in governance and management, on all organizational scales, into the foreseeable future.

The second, directly related to the first, is my preference for the Theory of Panarchy,[2] rather than of interregnum, as the conceptual framing of our current broken condition.

Interregnum, historically experienced as a gap of time in a linear process between one system of governance and another (as was, for example, the period of 206–202 BC in China, after the death of the final Qin emperor, when there was a contest to the throne until the accession of Liu Bang ushered in the Han Dynasty, or the time of unrest in Russia between 1598 and 1613 caused by power struggles between the Rurikid and Romanov dynasties), usually culminates with a return to order brought about by humans for humans. The theory of Panarchy embraces the possibility that humans are not the only drivers, nor the only managers, of change. According to C. S. Holling,[3] a Canadian ecologist, Panarchy 'is the structure in which systems, including those of nature (e.g., forests) and of humans (e.g., capitalism), as well as combined human–natural systems (e.g., institutions that govern natural resource use such as the Forest Service), are interlinked in continual adaptive cycles of growth, accumulation, restructuring, and renewal'. Holling suggests that these recurring dynamics in system adaptation are universal, take place at every level and affect individuals, communities and entire socio-political regions over periods from months to centuries.

The initial stage of the adaptive cycle, the exploitation and growth phase, is characterized by rapid growth, exploitation of new ecological conditions/markets and of temporarily plentiful resources. The system is diverse and resilient but low on internal connectivity. As it grows, the system becomes more stable and develops into the conservation phase of consolidation and accumulation. The competitive advantage enjoyed by the wasteful generalists/opportunists in the growth phase shifts to large and efficient specialists. Diversity and resilience decline as internal connectivity improves and, in the context of the economy, established firms become complacent and unresponsive to changing markets, new emerging technologies and new social needs. The system becomes more rigid and homogeneous and more vulnerable to shock.

According to Brian Walker and David Salt: 'the longer the conservation phase persists, the smaller the shock needed to end it'.[4] The third phase, release, can happen suddenly, as in the banking crisis of 2007, and bring many existing organizational structures to their knees. In the fourth, the reorganization phase, the chaos of release creates new opportunities for novelty and experimentation, many small agile alternatives emerge and the adaptation cycle repeats. If the collapse of the system is so severe that reorganization is no longer possible, the system exits the cycle altogether.

I would like to propose that, as men and nature are linked into one integrated system, and as we are experiencing a shock due to environmental crisis, the Panarchy theory offers a more suitable framework for examining current and future conditions than the linear, and human-controlled, interregnum.

Having thus defined my point of entry into this conversation, I can happily support Monika's proposition that we are now witnessing the beginnings of 'managing beyond the managerial elite', since the adaptation cycle creates conditions for innovation and, more importantly, for remembering what we already know worked before our current system imploded, including compassion and the Lévinasian moral impulse as suggested by Jerzy.

We are greatly aided and enabled to experiment with old and new forms of management by the new communication technologies. In his book *The Third Industrial Revolution*, Jeremy Rifkin[5] suggests that we are, in fact, entering the age of the revolution in his title, which relates closely to Jerzy's managerial revolution Mark III. Rifkin suggests that 'we are in the midst of a profound shift in the very way society is structured, away from hierarchical power and towards lateral power'.

Just as steam-powered technology enabled mass printing, which together brought about the First Industrial Revolution in the nineteenth century, so electrical communications (telegram and telephone), combined with oil-powered combustion engines, ushered in the Second Industrial Revolution in the twentieth century. The twenty-first century is embracing the Internet technologies and renewable energy, and these combined are 'laying the foundations for an emerging collaborative age'.[6] Rifkin foresees traditional, hierarchical structures, at all levels in organizations, giving way to distributed practice organized nodally across society and motivated not only by compassion and the moral impulse but also by rediscovery of biophilia,[7] defined by Edward Wilson as 'the connections that human beings subconsciously seek with the rest of life',[8] a rediscovery triggered by the current environmental threat.

So, to a large extent, Rifkin's Third Industrial Revolution supports the notion of the managerial revolution, and the age of collaboration is evidenced by the onset of crowd sourcing – 'turning to dispersed online communities, rather than the employees or suppliers, for a host of things, each contribution adding a small portion to the greater whole.'[9] Crowd Funding, Virtual Volunteering, Click Volunteers, Wikipedia, WikiHouse, Co-Production, Co-Making, Co-design, Occupy Wall Street and Occupy Management are all manifestations of this new, collaborative and dispersed phase in the adaptation cycle.

The desire for more collaborative working is also stimulating the rediscovery and growth of socially motivated organizational and governance structures, such as community interest companies, community enterprises, cooperatives, mutual societies, social firms and social enterprises. The desire to arrest the damage consumerism and greed have caused is also stimulating innovation on a neighbourhood and small-town scale, such as the Transition Movement and Cittaslow, but these are not transferring onto a city scale, despite many hopeful attempts.

My partial answer to Zygmunt's question, 'Supposing that we know what needs to be done, who is going . . .

to do it?', and to Monika's question of who the agents of change are, is that many individuals, community groups and neighbourhoods are experimenting (incentivized as much by the desire for a sustainable and just society as by disillusion with leadership and managers), to create the change that is needed. It is on a neighbourhood scale that some of the most inspiring civic experiments are being conducted, be it The Brixton Pound enabling local economy growth, or Isle of Eigg – the first community in Britain to be totally self -sufficient in renewable energy – or the severely deprived Thornton Estate in Hull, which is now running its own community services.

My answer is only partial because there is an issue, to which you have all alluded, of scaling up from individual organizations and neighbourhoods to a global community. It is true that cities are becoming increasingly powerful management units, aided once again by new technologies. SMART Cities and Big Data are informing management of resources, of traffic, and of an increasing number of challenges such as density, rising costs of energy and food, extreme weather events, and disaster response. All of these are stimulating extraordinary innovation to create facilitated adaptation and mitigation and to establish resilience that will make some cities stronger in the future than others.

Management of communication and other infrastructures such as transport stretches well beyond city boundaries. For infrastructures such as bio-diversity, the economy and ecology, regional scale is one that is regarded as essential to the wellbeing of a city. No sooner than our present government dismantled regional management structures, sub-regional and city regions concepts re-emerged in policy discourse in an attempt to manage the infrastructures that run beyond any one city.

Furthermore, cities are focused on themselves alone, and there are very few examples indeed of inspiring acts of generosity and collaboration between neighbouring cities. It is likely that, as we discover the benefits of the city state, we will also come to remember why these did not survive as distinct units of management.

It is not difficult to find examples of the deep inter-dependence between levels of management. Take, for example, the case reported on 8 January 2014 in all the media in the US, of New Jersey Governor Chris Christie's office punishing the insufficiently loyal mayor of Fort Lee by shutting down lanes to the George Washington Bridge, causing a 4-day-long traffic jam!

I suggest, therefore, that, as management of global resources is a global issue, neither cities nor city regions nor city states can do better in managing them than individual countries have done so far.

I would conclude that Occupy Management, Management III, distributed management and self-management are all essential ingredients of a general trend towards distributed practice, and that self-organized groups have an important role to play in future business and in the delivery of some local services and food and energy production, which will feed into city-scale management of all infrastructural matters. I would argue, however, that it is too early to give up on the state as it is still the appropriate institution, despite its short-comings, to tackle agreements on global matters. To Jerzy's quite justifiable concerns about the unaccount-ability of the powerful global elite, I would respond with a hopeful proposition that this edifice is crumbling

– more slowly than was hoped by some, but crumbling nevertheless, as we, society, are reconsidering our values. As Zygmunt often says, whilst refusing to suggest what the future might hold: 'We have a choice as to which way to go.' Is that not so?

Jerzy Kociatkiewicz Thank you, Irena, for introducing a whole array of ideas which should demand our attention and yet have remained unremarked upon. I agree with both you and Zygmunt that we have a choice as to which of our possible futures we shall realize, but, as your notion of Panarchy graphically suggests, the question of who 'we' are is both a difficult one to determine, and crucial for even starting to determine the possible or desirable choices.

Interestingly, work originating in the field of organizational sociology (if not, strictly speaking, management studies) offers perhaps the most promising toolkit for tackling issues of agency and interdependency in a world in which we can no longer pretend that human activity is the only activity worthy of attention and consideration. Beginning with a 1970s ethnographic study of a scientific laboratory,[10] Bruno Latour and a group of like-minded scholars developed what came to be known as actor-network theory.[11] The central idea of this approach, at least in my reading, lies in recognizing the multiplicity and variety of social actors involved in any complex issue affecting organizations or societies. Our every activity involves human and nonhuman participants (and quite often combinations and alliances between the two) – some recognizably sentient, some not. While early work in actor-network theory focused on high technology and scientific research settings where the important nonhuman actors were the scientific apparatuses, aircraft, trains or physical particles,[12] some newer studies use the theory for analysing environmental concerns, financial markets and the political constitution of our societies.[13] I would see the panarchic perspective as quite similar in situating humans as only a part – and not necessarily even the central one – of the problems we are currently facing.

As to whether such perspectives can allow us to envision (and move towards) models of management without managers (for I wholeheartedly agree with Monika's enthusiasm for such a concept), I would suggest that this depends on the triggers for significant changes (which we might see as a progression to the next stage in the ecological cycle, or as a more dramatic shift that changes the environment and the cycle itself). One of the hot topics of our times is the continuing growth of inequality, not only in terms of wealth and income, but also as regards access to resources and energy, to security and healthcare. The recent (and arguably ongoing) crisis seems only to have exacerbated the process. And yet, this happens alongside growing dissent and mounting evidence of the harm such polarization of society brings: Richard Wilkinson and Kate Pickett's *The Spirit Level*,[14] showing the destructive effects of wealth disparity for the privileged as well as the deprived has been one of the most hotly discussed books of the last few years. You, Zygmunt, have published your own views on the harm brought about by inequality in *Does the Richness of the Few Benefit Us All?*[15] A recent collection of interviews with CEOs and politicians[16] showed that they, too, largely feel the need (or the duty) to publicly condemn excessive wealth disparity. We are also witnessing a revival in the enthusiasm for cooperative organizations, both in their very traditional guises and in the new technological forms enumerated above by Irena. So far, the two trends (the growth of inequality and the indignation about it) run in parallel, serving as yet another example of the current social arrangements' loss of legitimacy.

It is here that I find the metaphor of interregnum particularly useful: without necessarily defining either the future monarchy or its subjects (be they human, nonhuman or a combination thereof), it points to the desire for – if not the inevitability of finding – new sources of legitimacy. In dynastic terms, we might yet see the return of previous claimants (I certainly would not mind seeing the word 'socialism' making a comeback in the mainstream discourse),[17] resurgence of the still regnant but increasingly delegitimized free market orthodoxy, or a radical new solution that builds on novel understandings, a new appreciation of our interdependence with the environment, on or new technologies. I hope that manager-less management can be part of such a solution, but I am far from confident that it will be.

Zygmunt Bauman Monika asks: is the revolution that Jerzy believes to be as badly needed as it is inescapable bound to consist in 'elimination of corporate structures of management and the actual empowerment of workers'?

Well, the topmost people hovering in the global 'space of flows'[18] – people who (let's face the facts) matter most, as do the opinions they voice in public as well as the practices that chime in unison with such opinions – insist that corporations belong neither to their employees, nor to the people who live within the reach of their operation and impact, but to their share-holders; and that the power to define their tasks and the actions pursuing them goes hand in hand with stock ownership. However harsh, callous, morally insensitive and altogether improper those opinions may sound, one can't deny outright their grounding in the current state of affairs. The postulated reform of the 'corporate structure of management' may well prove to be not much more than a cosmetic intervention as long as the exclusive right to set the agenda remains tied to that ownership.

Let me revisit Pierre Bourdieu, one of the most insightful and incisive sociologists of the last century, a past master of tearing up curtains woven of contrived and induced illusions. In a concise collection of essays and speeches under the joint title *Acts of Resistance*,[19] which amounts to his last will and testament – or his bequest of tasks left to us to undertake – he dedicated most of his attention to 'the euphemistic rhetoric which prevails in the money markets today' (see his speech in Freiburg in October 1996[20]). He criticized sharply the idea expressed by the President of the Bundesbank Tietmeyer, that the major – perhaps the sole – task of those who preside over the daily life of the economy and manage business units is to secure the 'confidence of investors' (as the President calls the stock owners, thus weaving the yarn of illusions into a curtain that needs to be torn in order to blaze the trail to the truth of the matter). According to President Tietmeyer, 'it is therefore necessary to restrain public spending and reduce taxation to a level that is acceptable in the long term, to reform the social welfare system, dismantle the rigidities in the labour market, since a new phase of growth will only be attained if we make an effort'.[21] Bourdieu unpacks that agglomeration of euphemisms: what is really proposed is that the economic entitlements of 'the investors' be awarded uncontested priority over the social entitlements of everybody else; employees need to be fired at will, cost-free; all in all, it is YOU, the managers, who must make an effort to force your employees to make more effort so that WE, 'the investors', may be confident of profits ... Is it 'all economy, stupid'? Or, rather, is it, after all, 'all economic power, stupid'?

I agree, reform of the corporate structure of management is among the most crucial and urgent tasks. But what about the corporate structure as such, of which management is but one specimen? Bourdieu warns repeatedly against ambush by economic determinism, whether of the Marxist or neo-liberal variety, which 'forbids responsibility and mobilization by cancelling out politics and imposing a whole set of unquestioned ends – maximum growth, competitiveness, productivity',[22] while giving itself 'the air of a message of liberation, through a whole series of lexical tricks around the idea of freedom, liberation, deregulation etc.'.[23]

To cut a long story short, what is covered up by all those 'lexical tricks' is the nature of the true choice: that between the confidence of the markets and the confidence of the people.

Now let me pause for a moment at Irena's promotion of the 'Panarchy' theory, instead of 'interregnum', as a right and proper cognitive frame in which to place our present, analyse its inner springs, grasp its role and meaning, even dare to surmise its sequel.

To start with, the idea of an 'interregnum' (in the new sense, stripped of its original monarchical connotations – the sense introduced by Antonio Gramsci[24] and recently resurrected, as well as updated, by Keith Tester[25]) has in my view a clear advantage of modesty and caution – avoiding the overconfidence and indeed presumptuousness of its 'Panarchy' competitor. Let me repeat: invoking the 'interregnum' when referring to a period of as yet unknown duration, currently lived-through by its insiders, manifests/conveys an awareness of what in the status quo haunts and repels those insiders and prompts them to seek its replacement; but it admits and signals simultaneously their ignorance about the form and shape such a replacement might eventually take. The state of interregnum is characterized by the tremendous difficulty, perhaps even impossibility, in guessing – let alone designing and planning with confidence and self-assurance – the sequel to the status quo. Emphatically, it rejects the idea of a future pre-determined, pre-ordained or pre-designed, leaving it wide open to similarly under-determined and as yet under-defined human choices – an idea that the theory of 'Panarchy', explicitly or implicitly, by design or by default, insinuates. While spelling out the reasons to run away from the status quo, representation of the state of affairs as one of 'interregnum' stays prudently cautious when it comes to predicting at what point that run might (let alone is bound to) grind to a halt.

Currently *en vogue*, the concept of 'Panarchy' is rooted in another version of the 'natural life-cycle' of civilizations, predetermining its course from its rise to its fall, from dawn to dusk, as if mimicking/replicating the itinerary of all living and therefore mortal organisms from birth to death. Such a view, of a relentless, unswerving and all but inexorable trajectory each successive civilization is doomed to follow has a long tradition in historiography and, more to the point, the philosophy of history, but about a century ago it was given a new stature and assured a steady – even if not a dominant – position in modern thought by Oswald Spengler in his adumbration of the 'Decline of the West'[26] – wherein he ascribed to every variety of civilization the unshakable, as well as unstoppable, succession of seasons that replicates the annual cycle.

Is this another incarnation of determinism, this time disguised as the iron law of civilization instead of the economy?

Well, to revisit Pierre Bourdieu once more: 'Social laws, economic laws and so on only take effect to the extent that people let them do so.'[27]

MK Exactly, and that is why I believe that we are now entering – or rather, re-entering – an era of reflection on what kind of laws and rules we are allowing to steer our lives. In a book I am writing now, I propose that we return to thinking of management – or, as you, Zygmunt, phrased it, an activity whose 'essential purpose ... has always been and remains the manipulation of probabilities of human conduct' – in terms of ethos. That ancient Greek idea embraces, on the one hand, place, and on the other, ethics, moral laws aimed at the diminishing of evil and increasing of good. The Czech economist and economic advisor to former President Václav Havel, Tomas Sedlacek, in his brilliant book *Economics of Good and Evil*,[28] argues that the meaning of economics is profoundly ethical: at heart, it is a science about good and evil. This is often completely ignored by the politicians and economists themselves, but even the formal and mathematical models it so proudly produced in recent decades have strong moral underpinnings, grow on a vision of society: what it should be, how people should treat one another and what they should believe in. The ideal conditions and the normative standards that economics abounds in spring from a desire to understand and to shape. The questions are, of course: what, by whom and for whom? These questions, often disregarded by mainstream economists, are of crucial importance and should be reflected upon consciously, to find our own place in the economic story of the world, which, as Sedlacek compellingly shows in his books, encompasses millennia. He retells and economically interprets tales such as that of Gilgamesh, biblical stories and those narrated by Enlightenment philosophers – including, of course, Adam Smith – showing that the ultimate meaning of economic reflection lies in ideas of goodness. Value is about not just finance, as we were led to believe in the most recent years of neo-liberal shortsightedness, but – as the term suggests – what we consider worthwhile, worth living for. A society where it is only profit that matters is deficient indeed; even though we are the richest civilization so far, we do not feel we have enough, we are overworked and wealth is distributed in a formidably unequal way, which Jerzy also addresses in his last reflection in our conversation. This state of things is a result of us losing touch with the meaning of it all. I agree with Sedlacek that we need to reclaim the moral dimension in our reflection upon society and its functions, as in the social science called economics. The role of economics is to provide knowledge about how to navigate: 'Economics should then mean the art of helmsmanship. The interaction of chaos and free will should not be understood as an obstacle (even if it appears as a stormy sea) but as a resource. Instead of trying to calm the sea down and directing it by threats of violence, one should instead learn how to steer *on it*.'[29] For management, I believe – which can take the shape of reflection, ideology and practice – not only a sense of direction, to be found in a consciousness of good and evil, is necessary, but also something more – a sense of place. Ethics and place is brought together in ethos.

The Polish management theorist Roman Batko in his revolutionary book *Golem, Midas, Avatar, Golden Calf*[30] calls urgently for a return to the ethos of social service, in which a sense of public management is to be found. The book presents four main ideas and, at the same time, eras in public management, which Batko describes with the help of striking metaphors. Golem is the classic bureaucracy of the early twentieth century – on the one hand, efficient and standardized, and, on the other, soulless, occasionally even systemically homicidal – as you, Zygmunt, so pertinently described in *Modernity and the Holocaust*.[31] Midas is the incarnation of the public sector shaped in the image of the corporate world. Under the banner of New Public Management, the public sphere was to be made truly effective and even profitable, with all the traditional dysfunctional evils banned once and for all. However, the corporate-imitation public organization became, if possible, even more monstrous and inhuman than its role model. While not directly organizing mass murder, as its predecessor did, it disdainfully and unfeelingly condoned human suffering, injustice and misery. The public organization of this era became yet another servant of capital, extolling economic values only, and oblivious to its original goals as a tool for making a difference in society and working for the less privileged, for justice and peace. Avatar is another embodiment of the public organization, intended as the ultimate cost-effective and user-friendly, 'lean' version of public administration for everyone. Functions of public organizations would be accessible via the Internet, in a comprehensible technological interface. In reality, it not only fails to fulfil its promises, but becomes an even more inhuman, depersonalized and dismal organization – or, perhaps, a colossal robot. Finally, the Golden Calf is a typically Polish version of the public sphere, in which religious institutions try to shape or take over functions of the organizations traditionally belonging to state or local governments. The Catholic Church in Poland is, in particular, eager to undertake such endeavours, with the justification that the public sphere needs some moral engagement. However, in reality, such practices do not bring back the sacred into the profane organization but, rather, profane the sacred and instigate a cult of its own structures, hierarchies and politics. Roman Batko claims that there is no solution to the dilemma – it is impossible to eliminate the pathologies that are inherent to and devastate the public sector. But there is something that can be done, if the public organization is to be brought back to life: bring it back its soul, its meaning – the ethos of public service. In the Golem of the legend of Prague, who was created by the Rabbi Jehuda Löw ben Becalel to protect the persecuted Jewish community but, devoid of a soul, became its tormentor instead, because an inscription placed inside his mouth lost one letter – instead of *emet* ('truth') he carried the word *met* ('death'). So the public organization, devoid of its truth – which is an offshoot of the activity of its ethos – carries only different images of death: efficacy, cost-effectiveness and instrumentality. The ethos of the public organization is public service, care about others and public good, not in an abstract but an embodied and emplaced sense. This is, according to the author, what humanistic management in the public sector should regard as its roots and aims.

Irena, Zygmunt and Jerzy, which laws and ethoses do you believe are able to regulate a future world? In other words, how can the global and the local be organized, by whom and for whom? Going back to Jerzy's musings, how can this reorganization deal with the injustices of our world? Do you believe in a come-back for socialism, a resurgence of the free market economy or something radically new? But that is a question for a new chapter of our conversation.

3

The organization of the global and the local

Irena Bauman Thank you, Jerzy, for urging us to consider the growth of inequality as one of the most challenging social issues for society to manage in the future, and to Monika for restating the propositions from Tomas Sedlacek that the meaning of economics is profoundly ethical, and that at heart it is a science about good and evil. I will take these as starting points for considering Monika's questions about the laws and ethos that may regulate a future world.

Zygmunt ends his succinct and beautifully crafted essay *Does the Richness of the Few Benefit Us All?* with an observation validated by historic events: 'It seems that one needs catastrophes to happen in order to recognize and admit (retrospectively alas, only retrospectively . . .) their coming.'[1]

This observation is particularly chilling in the context of managing the future since we are, for the first time in human history, facing a number of existential threats. These extinction-level man-made risks have been identified by the newly constituted Centre for the Study of

Existential Risk at the University of Cambridge as the products of four key developments: the advancement of artificial intelligence, the development of biotechnology and artificial life, the progress of nanotechnology, and the possible extreme effects of anthropogenic climate change.

In this new context of colossal catastrophes ahead, the principle that positive change can only be triggered by those catastrophes is unpalatable if we want civilization to continue.

The action now required is a re-definition of *true choice*, from that identified by Zygmunt as 'between the confidence of the markets and the confidence of the people' to one already captured by the most famous six words in the history of literature: *To be or not to be?*

It is this choice, coupled with the failure of the free market and consumerism to deliver wellbeing and happiness identified by Monika, which may accelerate us into what Jerzy phrased 'the return of previous claimants' to dislodge the ruling order described by the economist E. F. Schumacher as 'anonymous companies or megalomaniac governments which pretend to themselves that the whole universe is their legitimate quarry'.[2] It is also this choice that gives legitimacy to the abundance of ideas and experiments, on all scales and across the whole world, regarding managing ourselves differently.

Building on the premise put forward by Schumacher that 'there is wisdom in smallness if only on account of the smallness and patchiness of human knowledge, which relies on experiment far more than on understanding',[3] I would argue that there is now patchy evidence of patchy corrective actions designed to prevent further catastrophes, and of management systems and organizational structures adapting in support of changing social values, and that the pace of this change is accelerating – although still only amongst early adopters.

That we are in a period of corrective action cannot be denied. Just in the last few months, an LSE report revealed that banks have been fined £3.5 billion for Libor rate rigging. In January 2014, it was confirmed that the banks were fined the sum of £10 billion for mis-selling of payment protection insurance, raising the total of this fine to £20 billion. Again in January 2014, the EU introduced a cap on bankers' bonuses, and, more significantly, shifted the decision-making for fixing the level of bonuses from the closed remuneration committees to the stakeholders, thus changing the governance structure. The agreement was reached during eight hours of intense talks in Brussels between members of the European Parliament, the European Commission and representatives of the bloc's twenty-seven governments.[4] Othmar Karas, the European Parliament's chief negotiator, said: 'For the first time in the history of EU financial market regulation, we will cap bankers' bonuses.'[5]

Also in 2014, the Basel Committee, a powerful group of bank regulators that meets regularly to agree risk management rules that affect every bank on the planet, introduced a new set of financial regulations said to be 'the most important global initiative to learn the lessons of the 2008 banking crisis and correct them'[6] (note the reference to the 'global').

Even Zygmunt's 'topmost people hovering in the global "space of flows"' are feeling the tides of change. The CEOs of Barclays Bank, RBS and the utilities company Centrica all turned down their substantial bonuses under the pressure of public opinion.

The voluntary management of redistribution, philanthropy, is making a comeback since 2008, with America's wealthiest donors giving more than £2.1 billion to charity in 2013, the largest donation of 18 million shares in Facebook being made by Mark Zuckerberg to the Silicon Valley Community Foundation.[7] Again in January 2014, the Socialist People's Party in Denmark resigned from the government coalition in support of the public outcry against the government's decision to sell 19% per cent of the shares in government-owned renewable energy company DONG to Goldman Sachs.[8]

These are, admittedly, but isolated events in a sea of less happy ones, but such events are early indications of a profound change in social values. As Jerzy suggests, there is 'growing dissent and mounting evidence of the harm [from] polarization of society', and many great minds are working across different scales of governance to define a new future based on social and intergenerational justice and a sustainable use of resources, and the most powerful concept that binds them all is that of: 'redistribution'. In their influential *How Much is Enough?*, Robert and Edward Skidelsky[9] re-examine the possibility of 'The Good Life', as conceived by Aristotle and developed by economists ever since, which starts with the consideration not of social justice, but of the balance of work and leisure to satisfy individual needs: 'Imagine a world in which most people work only fifteen hours a week. They would be paid as much as, or even more than, they now are, because the fruit of their labour would be distributed more evenly across society.'[10] Redistribution of income, wealth and decision-making is central also to the New Economics Foundation (NEF) report 'The Great Transition', in which they suggest a raft of changes including creation of a Citizens' Endowment to provide a basic income for all, and argue for greater localization, as decisions are best made on as local a scale as possible.

The theme of redistribution is reaching beyond the words of theorists through ever more frequent experiments and movements on the ground. Transition Network, a charitable organization whose role is to inspire, encourage, connect, support and train communities as they self-organize, creating initiatives that rebuild resilience and reduce CO_2 emissions through sharing and collective action, has sprouted initiatives all over the world since 2009. CittaSlow, the movement that aims to protect distinctive local economies against global homogenizing through citizen involvement in local governance, has spread to 147 towns in 24 countries.

So, in response to Monika's question, and on the assumption that society can stay in control of its own destiny – which is by no means certain – I would argue that existential risks are already becoming the main driver of positive social change, and that the move towards a more desirable society can be organized through reconfiguration of existing hierarchical management to one of collective stewardship, accompanied by a shift in mode of operation from institutional control to institutional facilitation, and from competition to cooperation, all of it underpinned by shared values of humility and social and environmental justice – that is, values shaping structures, not the other way round.

As to the question of who would do all this, the possible answer is that everyone has a part to play – from each according to his ability, to each according to his needs is a welcomed return claimant, an essential premise of *collective stewardship*. Such stewardship also requires taking responsibility for the consequences of our own actions.

Now it is my turn to ask a question: what has each one of us redistributed lately?

Zygmunt Bauman   Yes, 'everyone *has* a part to play' – but *will* everyone carry out their role? Or maybe some of us will, not all (in a species as variegated as ours that is highly unlikely, perhaps inconceivable), but will this be enough to re-set the rules of the game? The odds seem to be set against such a re-setting – considering the depth of the seldom-articulated, yet daily and commonly practised, presumptions that underpin our vision of the world as well as our life strategies.

As W. I. Thomas and Florian Znaniecki[11] memorably observed, if humans define situations as real, they are real in their consequences. Whereas, in the words of J. M. Coetzee, an exceptionally acute observer of our ways and means of cohabiting (see his *Diary of a Bad Year*[12]), behind the justification

> of unceasing business lie assumptions that no longer need to be articulated, so self-evidently true do they seem: that each person on earth must belong to one nation or another and operate within one or another national economy; that these national economies are in competition with one another . . . Economic activity as a race . . . has no finishing line and therefore no natural end. The runner's sole goal is

to get in front and stay there. The question of why life must be likened to a race, or of why the national economies must race against one another rather than going for a comradely jog together, for the sake of their health, is not raised.[13]

This is the situation that we define as real, and whose reality we daily reproduce and reinforce through the way we live our lives: through what we believe to be the goals worth pursuing and through the way in which we pursue them. The Basel Committee, to whose initiatives you, Irena, refer, would hardly consider the situation described by Coetzee anything less than self-evident; what the Committee helmspeople seek to impose on 'risk managers' is to draw 'lessons from the 2008 banking crisis and correct them', in order to salvage from perdition that 'self-evident reality of the race' that the recklessness and instant-profit-guided myopia of banks exposed to the danger of dissipating. Does this swallow, or even a whole flight of such swallows, make a summer? The purpose, to the servicing of which banks are prodded to return by learning their lessons, is not, after all, a 'good life' according to any definition other than that of constantly rising dividends for 'global investors'. That purpose is the restoration of the competitiveness that the banks – focused on the market value of stocks and the bonuses and dividends of their owners – once allowed to follow their own logic, were about to destroy. Are those measures indeed, as you surmise and suggest, invented and promoted with the intention of shifting the 'mode of operation' 'from *institutional control* to *institutional facilitation*', and 'from *competition* to *cooperation*, all of it underpinned by shared values of humility and social and environmental justice', or in the hope of mitigating the impact of shocks and so playing down the urgency and the depth of needed reform? Were they not, at the end of the day, attempts to protect the system against brash and rash operators? And isn't the 'patchiness' of the 'evidence of patchy corrective actions designed to prevent further catastrophes', which you so rightly note, a manifestation of the wish to prevent – or at least put off and postpone – major surgery with a series of minor, and consolingly innocuous, cosmetic interventions?

But major surgery is unavoidable as far as the resources of the planet, which are steadily nearing exhaustion, are concerned, in parallel with the steadily rising numbers of those with a claim to them. The challenge we confront is not the question of whose legitimate quarry our shared universe is or ought to be, but the most urgent demand to stop treating that universe as a quarry – to recall Lewis Mumford's old precept and warning, to turn from the 'mining' worldview, posture and strategy to their 'farming' counterparts:

> The miner's notion of value, like the financier's, tends to be a purely abstract and quantitative one. Does the defect arise out of the fact that every other type of primitive environment contains food, something that may be immediately translated into life – game, berries, mushrooms, maple-sap, nuts, sheep, corn, fish – while the miner's environment alone is – salt and saccharin aside – not only completely inorganic but completely inedible?[14]

He continues: 'The miner works, not for love or for nourishment, but to "make his pile." The classic curse of Midas became perhaps the dominant characteristic of the modern machine: whatever it touched was turned to gold and iron, and the machine was permitted to exist only where gold and iron could serve as foundation.'[15] Meeting that challenge and standing up to it would have to affect not only the behaviour of the 'anonymous companies or megalomaniac governments', but the way of being-in-the-world for us all. We ought to be prepared to pay the high costs of transition. Among the costs, the ideas that the uninterrupted rise of GNP is the universal all-purpose cure for all and any social ills and problems, while perpetually intensifying shopping activity is what the human right to the pursuit of happiness requires, are bound to be found among the most painful sacrifices.

Mumford ought to be remembered for his many acute and prophetic observations, acquiring today even more weight than they carried when written down. For instance, he wrote (In *Values for Survival*):

> If we are to create balanced human beings, capable of entering into world-wide co-operation with all other men of good will – and that is the supreme task of our generation, and the foundation of all its other potential achievements – we must give as much weight to the arousal of the emotions and to the expression of moral and esthetic values as we now give to science, to invention, to practical organization. One without the other is impotent.[16]

And for his declaration of faith, he said: 'I'm a pessimist about probabilities, I'm an optimist about possibilities.'[17]

It is there that the fundamental question of 'who will do it' acquires its awesome poignancy. Because extant companies, anonymous or not, and extant governments, megalomaniac or not – the only instruments we possess to recycle collective intentions into collective actions – seem (and are!) singularly unfit and utterly unlikely to inscribe the above sacrifices on their banners, and least of all to recycle the slogans into deeds. Companies are made unfit by the fear of losing their clients; governments by the fear of losing their electors.

Jerzy Kociatkiewicz Perhaps because of the bias of my self-identification as an organization-theorist, I do not think your question, Irena, regarding our personal efforts at redistribution, is a particularly relevant one for our conversation – I believe that one of the primary reasons that human beings invented organizations was to allow for actions that are beyond the scope of the individual, whether concerning production or distribution. Consequently, I see our roles of redistributors as indelibly bound to our activities as members of organizations – though, of course, these organizations can range in size and significance from the smallest circles of friends to nation-states and global corporations. In one of Adam Smith's most often-quoted passages, he noted that 'It is not from the benevolence of the butcher, the brewer, or the baker that we expect our dinner, but from their regard to their own interest.' While the line is often interpreted to imply that the magic of the free market transforms selfish desires into the common good (turning business acumen into moral virtue), I think the more important lesson (that still does not turn into over-interpretation) is that social institutions and frameworks of cooperation – in other words, organizations, of which the nation-states were the most important ones for Smith – are needed in order to create shared benefits. A quarter of a millennium later, the notion seems to hold true for us as well.

Thus, I see my own involvement in redistribution as vested in the organization to which I devote the majority

of my time – the university, which I still think offers
some of the best hopes for convincing 'everyone' to
play their part, through the building of and participation in social institutions and organizational networks
rather than through individual charity. There are, of
course, severe dangers in this optimistic vision, the chief
of which are the attempts to cast university education
as an individual investment to be recouped through
future career earnings. In the current British system,
this metaphor is taken quite literally, as student fees,
covered by the government, are expected to be repaid
by students from their earnings following graduation.
This individualized, investment-centred approach to
education is acknowledged and encouraged by universities themselves, as in this advice to students provided by
the University of Edinburgh (other university websites
and brochures contain similar sentiments): 'One of the
main reasons students choose to study at university is to
enhance their career prospects. This becomes increasingly important in view of rising costs of education
and levels of debt on graduation, so individuals want
to ensure it has been money well spent.'[18] Yet, as you,
Zygmunt, have pointed out so many times, ours are
times of uncertainty and chance, and the most universities have to offer to a canny individual is a ticket for
the employment market lottery (where, it needs to be
noted, no prize is certain and all awards are revocable).
This is neatly summed up by the notion of employability (now featured in university rankings and appearing
prominently in university promotional materials, and
espoused by government reports as a key component of
higher education): the generalized suitability for becoming employed, which carries no promises of actual work

and entirely bypasses the question of interest, fulfilment or relevance to be found in the positions for which one might be deemed employable.

Reflecting, as long ago as 1985, about the continued dizzying discrepancy between competing economic predictions and relative paucity of accurate auguries, Donald McCloskey[19] postulated that economics should be understood primarily as a toolkit for historical investigation, readily able to explain events in the past while offering little concrete advice about the future of complex economic systems. As the conditions of liquid modernity reach ever more intimately into individual lives, career counsellors find themselves in similar straits to predictive economists: the lives of their charges are too volatile, too unpredictable and too complex for traditional career plans to have any reasonable chances of realization. Thus, Jim Bright and Robert Pryor, writing twenty years after McCloskey, came to strikingly similar conclusions in their own field of interest, proposing that career counselling should focus on explaining the continuing turbulences in clients' lives rather than offering inevitably improbable plans and goals: 'The emphasis here is on understanding processes and influences and how these have shaped and continue to shape individuals' experience of the world. Narrative counselling techniques emphasize the role of story construction in understanding careers. . . . Narrative provides a vehicle for understanding the motive processes in a person's career.'[20] Thus, it is not career chances that I hope the universities will be redistributing, as that simply entails participation in a competitive race destined to generate ever more numerous hordes of losers, facing a world where no skillset offers a secure route to employment.

For the first time in living memory, the whole class of graduates faces a high probability – almost a certainty – of ad-hoc, temporary, insecure and part-time jobs, unpaid 'trainee' pseudo-jobs deceitfully re-branded 'practices' – all considerably below their acquired skills, and eons below the level of their expectations; or of a stretch of unemployment lasting longer than it will take for the next class of graduates to add their names to the already uncannily long job-centre waiting lists.[21]

On the other hand, I still believe in the potential for universities to redistribute knowledge, critical reflection, and ideas for social change, though of course these topics strain the limits of the resource metaphor: they all increase rather than deplete through sharing and discussion. But it is also the answer to the question of who might (I'm wary of the 'will') do it – that is, who will change the world, whether through revolution or evolution: I look with hope towards our students who, in my experience, are rather sceptical about the promises of success through employability and flexibility.

Monika Kostera In answer to Irena's question – and repeating Jerzy's answer – I do not think that redistribution is my job, or the job of any individual. A few days ago, when I was walking in the city in the torrential rain we are having in Britain this winter, I saw a seller of the *Big Issue*, completely soaked, walking despondently up and down his patch, rather desperately trying to sell an issue of the journal. I bought one, which was pretty wet, which did not matter much as I had already bought an issue earlier the same week, from another distributor. I did it out of compassion and respect for the seller, but felt no gratitude that I had been able to make a difference or help him in his situation – instead, I felt an immense sadness and an anger at the state that is failing so miserably, and also nowadays so self-righteously, its most fundamental obligations towards society. As you, Zygmunt, so many times have repeated, society is only as strong as its weakest link, and in that the task of the government is not unlike the duty of the engineer constructing bridges – to make sure that the whole structure holds, or, in the case of the state, to see to it that all members of society have a decent fundamental way to make a living. Individuals should not, in my opinion, have any decisive authority in deciding who should live or not, who should eat and who not, who should get a life-saving operation and who should go without. Homeless people should be able to get by on centrally or locally redistributed funds, and, if they then like, they could sell the *Big Issue* or, even better, a journal authored and run by homeless people, to earn extra money and to feel fruitfully employed. It would then be my choice, and the choice of other passers-by, whether to buy a copy or not, whether to drop 50 pence into a street musician's hat or walk away unmoved. The responsibility for these people should be shared by all in solidarity – and that is a fundamental task of government. This also helps the deprived to preserve their dignity and perhaps encourages some to think of their future in brighter tones, considering taking up education or making some other plans. People usually plan ahead and are willing to learn if they feel secure and if they have a sense of basic dignity, not having to beg or throw themselves on other individuals' mercy. Yet, in so many countries these days, this function of the state is failing utterly, and it is a black irony that, at the same time, as Tomas Sedlacek[22] pointed out, ours is the richest society in known human history. Globally, humanity disposes of resources it has never before had access to. Despite this, poverty and misery are what the lot of most of the inhabitants of our planet is closest to. It is not a failure of the economy. It is a failure of management on the macro level. My conjecture is, then, that change management on this level has to be as profound and radical as the most all-encompassing instances of change management – it is my belief that governments should learn from theories of change management.

In the management literature, we often encounter descriptions of different modes of change. For example, let us consider a simple but interesting typology, distinguishing between two such basic modes. Morphostasis,[23] or first-order change,[24] is a process which does not affect the foundations of the system, particularly the institutions that affect its abilities to make sense of reality. The second mode, morphogenesis, or second-order change, is one entering into the deepest levels, involving the most taken-for-granted cultural assumptions – the interpretive schemes used as milestones in all organizational endeavours. When a system undergoes such a deep process of change, the organization first and foremost becomes reinterpreted and re-conceived by management and its participants. This is the basis for a successful organizational metamorphosis. What then must follow in order for the whole process to be completed are structural and material reconfigurations. These can take one of two shapes: either evolution (incrementalism), relatively peaceful and slow, or revolution, occurring relatively fast and causing discontinuity.[25]

Revolutionary change in itself does not necessarily imply morphogenesis. Cultural foundations endure, revolutions are reinterpreted in terms of old cultural patterns; labels and surface may change (and so can artifacts from both the economic and political spheres), but the essence (cultural assumptions) remains the same.[26]

So, second-order change or morphogenesis becomes possible when, first of all, a radical questioning of the main cultural institutions is followed by a vision for change, and then this vision is acted upon, organized to actually happen. As Barbara Czarniawska aptly put it, 'change can take place when someone – or some group – acts as if the rules of the future applied today, or *as if the change had already taken place*'.[27] The rationality of tomorrow, not the one of today, would have to be followed and produced by the actors of today. During the interregnum, no one knows for sure which these are, and we increasingly observe 'alternative scenarios' or even 'alternative realities', which causes massive confusion and is, perhaps, one of the main driving forces in the emergence of so many fundamentalist revivals in our times: the human being is, primarily, a sense-making creature and all of his or her endeavours are made possible only if he or she succeeds in making sense of bits of the world linked to what he or she wishes to do.[28] We will perhaps live in a world where there is a polyphony of 'multiple realities, where organizations are both major producers and the main products of these realities',[29] and the task of the good manager is, first and foremost, to make sense of this uncomforting and paralysing multitude by a courageous and visionary *management of meaning*.[30]

ZB Chinese folk wisdom avers that if you plan for a year, you should sow corn; if for a dozen years, you should plant a tree; and if for a hundred years – educate people . . . But who would be keen to plan nowadays for a hundred years ahead – let alone who is sufficiently potent to put such a plan effectively into operation? The time-horizon of the political class is locked in the brief interval between elections. The time-horizon of the financial and economic class is confined to the (the shorter, the better) span between two successive 'killings'. The time-horizon of the intellectual elite gathered inside the walls of Academia seldom stretches beyond the next round of grant distribution and/or the next year's student-recruitment exercise. Prospective recruits are tempted with the promise of high salaries closely following their graduation day: an appeal is made, as in the prospectus quoted by Jerzy, to a supposed chance of 'enhancing their career prospects'. Their desire of a meaningful, creative and gratifying life, the desire to add to the world rather than to detract from it, is not addressed, let alone beefed up. The evolution of the species – which ran, roughly speaking, from the plankton-like, day-to-day and hour-by-hour, from-hand-to-mouth existence, to the refitting/restructuring/fixing of the human habitat – seems to be currently running back to a plankton-style adjustment to the haphazard, unpredictable and uncontrollable vagaries of a systematically exploited, impoverished and disabled environment; and from the labour invested in rendering the world malleable, pliable and submissive to human control, all the way to the 'flexibility' (read: spinelessness, programmatic un-fixity) of humans.

Jerzy hits the bull's eye when suggesting: 'one of the

primary reasons that human beings invented organizations was to allow for actions that are beyond the scope of the individual'. Planning far ahead is clearly among those actions beyond the scope of the individual imagination and power to act, and one of the prime *raisons d'être* of organizations (those, so to speak, 'communities-by-design', or contrived communities, as distinct from communities: those, so to speak, 'organizations-by-default', or spontaneous organizations; both types of supra-individual formations engaged in coordinating individual human actions – in other words, in manipulating the probabilities of their choices). If management in the sense of manipulating the probabilities of human conduct, is a sine-qua-non, un-detachable attribute to all collective action, then effective planning far ahead, beyond the scope of individual resourcefulness, is an un-detachable task of all management. That task, however, has been by and large abandoned – together with the abandoning of the managed to their limited resources and vision. The function of managing has increasingly shrunk to the creaming-off of the results of diffuse and scattered individual undertakings. Induced individual rivalry and competition now occupy the place once allocated to the objectives set and pursued by organized long-term planning.

To return to the line of thought sketched above: with the network of interdependence stretching far beyond the reach of the integrating/coordinating tools available to communities – the 'natural' communities – their replacement/supplementation by organizations – the potentially (and perhaps in their original intention) 'artificial communities', communities-by-design – is in all probability as unavoidable as it is desirable. Monika is absolutely right to postulate that individuals should not 'have any decisive authority in deciding who should live or not, who should eat and who not, who should get a life-saving operation and who should go without'. But contemporary organizations run according to the current managerial philosophy which has stopped well short of developing an instrument capable of tackling the communal function, which both Irena – when she focuses on distribution – and Monika – when she protests against the abandoning of the homeless to peddling the *Big Issue* – have in mind. More and more, the contemporary organization turns into an incubator for rivalry and cut-throat competition. When it comes to the social emotions of the solidarity-mutuality-loyalty-cooperation-purpose-sharing kind, it is a singularly infertile soil for planting and growing them – let alone making them thrive.

4

Utopian hopes

Jerzy Kociatkiewicz Trying to dilute the myriad ideas fluttering through the conversation (some staying for a longer time, some only just implied) into a proposed topic for the next round of musings, I am struck by the notion of hope which has, in its various guises, appeared time and again in our attempts to make sense of the actual and expected changes around us. This is not unexpected, as our home disciplines of sociology, management and architecture are all deeply entangled in possibilities of improving the social world (as well as full of critical voices questioning that possibility). I would thus like to up the ante and ask you about the ultimate horizon of hope – your visions of utopia, that fabled place we are always trying to strive towards. It seems that the notion of utopia has reappeared in public and academic thought, from Fredric Jameson's[1] revival of utopia as crucial for understanding our contemporary world and culture, through the very utopian strivings of participants in the Arab spring, the recent revolution in Ukraine and numerous protest actions across the globe, to the violent utopian visions of religious and nationalist fundamentalisms in all their guises. The idea of hope seems relevant again, with claims of 'there-is-no-alternative' and the end of history appearing quaintly obsolete. Zygmunt, you have spoken about utopia on a number of different occasions; let me bring back just two of your statements. In *Socialism: The Active Utopia*, you wrote:

> I think social life cannot in fact be understood unless due attention is paid to the immense role played by utopia. Utopias share with the totality of culture the quality – to paraphrase Santayana – of a knife with the edge pressed against the future. They constantly cause the reaction of the future with the present, and thereby produce the compound known as human history.[2]

Some thirty years later, you noted that the privatization of fates and life choices subsumed under the notion of searching for individual happiness threatened the very notion of utopia, understood, ever since Plato and Thomas More, as a collective enterprise:

> Unlike the utopian model of good life, happiness is thought of as an aim to be pursued individually, and as a series of happy moments succeeding each other – not as a steady state. . . . In the transgressive imagination of liquid modernity the 'place' (whether physical or social) has been replaced by the unending sequence of new beginnings, inconsequentiality of deeds has been substituted for fixity of order, and the desire of a different today has elbowed out concern with a better tomorrow.[3]

As is usual in reading your work, I find myself agreeing with both of these statements even as they seem to lead in opposite directions (thankfully, the complexity of the human condition not only allows for, but even welcomes, paradoxes much more stark than this). But I would like you all to chip in on the idea of utopias (and their dystopian cousins), and their relevance to our current situation.

Zygmunt Bauman You may remember that young Foucault broke into the learned attention of the scholarly establishment with the idea of 'discursive formation', meant to replace the concept of 'paradigm' with which at that time Thomas Kuhn[4] caught and firmly held the minds and hearts of social scientists – glad and grateful to have been offered a chance to lift their diffuse and unspecified unease to the noble rank of a scientific revolution. Unlike Kuhn's 'paradigm', discursive formation did not stand by the logical cohesion of the interpretations it inspired, and fall because of an unmanageable volume of 'anomalies' that it inadvertently generated (that is, the empirical data that cast in doubt, defied and sapped those interpretations because the current paradigm could not account for them). Foucault's *discursive formation*[5] visualized reality as a sort of matrix allowing a great number of diverse permutations: like that reality, it allowed for contradictions. The capability of producing mutually contradictory sentences was, according to Foucault, the discursive formations' indelible mark, indeed their constitutive feature. As I see no reason to question Foucault's insight, I fully agree with your observation that 'the complexity of the human condition not only allows for, but even welcomes, paradoxes much more stark than this'.

But to return to your tremendously important questions concerning our present-day plight and the prospects for 'utopianist' thinking: let me start by recalling this time an English, rather than Chinese, proverb: one that notices – moodily – that every man runs for himself, and the Devil takes the hindmost. Or the observation from John Kenneth Galbraith, who, having looked around our world with an exquisitely well-trained, eagle-sharp eye, found in it *private opulence* cohabiting with *public squalor*[6] – public space having been reduced to the status of a rubbish tip for the trash and litter turned out by the commotion aimed at building and fortifying enclosures of opulence. As he himself pointed out in the same study: the greater the wealth, the thicker will be the dirt.

Well, utopia did return from its temporary settlement in the 'recreation and entertainment' holiday camp to (as Jerzy rightly observes) reappear 'in public and academic thought'. But it returned in a guise sharply distinct from the one it wore before its exile from those thoughts. Before its temporary exile, it used to carry all the birth marks of a gardener's predispositions. Like gardens, those designs guiding and ordering the gardener's vocation, that utopia was a vision of ultimate harmony in which every insider-plant had its own dignified and praiseworthy slot allocated, while all possible blots on the landscape were conspicuous solely by their absence. No nook or cranny was left unattended and unscrutinized. Gardeners' utopias were visions of perfect *totality* – the quality of its parts coming a (sometimes distant) second, as its derivative and after-effect. You would hardly find all that, however, among the returnees from exile.

The utopias of our times, just like their older namesakes, are visions of a better world. But this time it is a vision of a fragmented – deregulated – world, individualized and privatized. In other words, it reincarnates as a hunters', not a gardeners', utopia. There is little room there for care for the totality, for a harmonious whole, for the right and proper location for all and any insider. It is a 'winner take all' utopia of hunters, concerned as they are, each one of them, with the contents of his hunting bag at the end of the hunting day, and giving little – if any – thought to the predicament of the less dexterous, less sharp-eyed huntsmen or detractors from shooting and killing – let alone to how much, if anything at all, of the game might survive the hunt. Hunters' utopia is not a vision of a perfect *world*. It is a vision of a perfect (private) spot carved out and protected against hopelessly imperfect and repellent surroundings: of a relatively convenient, comfortable and secure niche to be cut out, individually, from the essentially and irreparably awkward, prickly and insecure world. And, once cut out, it is to be fenced off tightly, impermeably, from the wilderness doomed to decay.

Joseph de Maistre[7] suggested once, in passing, that each society has a ruler it deserves. We could say that each society also has utopias it deserves. Our utopias fit a world that allots its material and spiritual prizes according to the size of the last killing.

Irena Bauman I heard it said somewhere that a person is only truly dead and gone when his or her name is spoken for the last time in the world. So it must be with the passage of all things, but on this basis the gardeners' utopia of *life in balance* is far from dead. On the contrary, its name is spoken louder than ever – we have not forgotten such a possibility and the human race has not lost its deep desire for it. If anything the longing for it intensifies with rising awareness that the life of consumption is leading us towards a futile pursuit:

Money that you don't have;
To spend on things that you don't need;
To create an impression that won't last;
On people that you don't care about.[8]

Current dystopias are based on the premise that social values will not change, and that we will continue to enjoy our privileges and entitlements, to take and to use more than our fair share just because we can. The We to which I am referring in this case are the comfortable middle classes and not just the super-rich. (Note to interlocutors and readers: please take a moment away from your busy schedules to test your sense of entitlement – visit the unoccupied rooms in your houses and consider whether you would ever miss the many objects accumulated in them. You may also reflect on the amount of food that you have binned this week and the hours that your car, or cars, stood idle outside your front door and on the unproductive time you have spent in unsuccessful pursuits of grants and projects, and whether it is possible to redistribute more than just the loose change in your pocket. What would be the real loss if we were to live without waste: goods or our entitlement to them?)

Currently 20 per cent of the world's population is consuming 80 per cent of the world's resources, and collectively we are consuming twice as much as the Earth can sustain. In *Collapse: How Societies Choose to Fail and Succeed*, Jared Diamond,[9] Professor of Geography at the University of California, Los Angeles (allegedly 'America's best-known geographer'), examined civilizations such as those of the Norse, Rapa Nui, Inuit, Maya and others that collapsed in the past, and suggests that the reasons why some thrived and others perished are ecological rather than cultural.

More precisely, he identified five possible contributing factors to putative environmental collapse and suggests that four of those sets of factors – environmental damage, climate change, hostile neighbours and friendly trade partners – may or may not prove significant for a particular society, whilst the fifth set of factors – the society's response to its environmental problems – always proves significant.

In his article 'The Unholy Trinity, Plus One',[10] Jim Dator from the Institute of Alternative Futures in Florida suggested four alternative futures for us, each determined by the actions we – society – decide to take now. The first option is keep the economy growing, which means business as usual and a continuation of a fossil-fuel-based economy. This could eventually lead to scenario two, which he calls 'severe energy, environmental and economic challenges', with collapsing society as a potential and most extreme outcome. The refuted and mocked propositions made by the most uncompromising of climate change scientists, James Lovelock,[11] come true: by 2020, extreme weather will be the norm, causing global devastation; by 2040, much of Europe will be Saharan, and parts of London will be underwater.

'Transformational visions' is a third scenario in which we find solutions to current challenges, predominantly through the application of new technologies and genetic modification. In the fourth scenario, 'Towards disciplined, evolvable (sustainable) societies', we return to living within our means.

Most of us, individuals as well as organizations, are reluctant to dwell on dystopian futures mainly because they are frightening and so make us anxious, but also because immediate action and a long-term vision are needed to combat the threats, and these are commodities in short supply, especially among men and women of power. These supreme hunters are resorting instead to sceptical denial.

While the evidence has convinced many of the need to take action, others, many of them influential, have been more reluctant. Well documented is the shifting sequence of 'climate sceptics'' arguments in response to global warming: the 'climate isn't changing' . . . 'it is changing but it is not us' . . . 'it is us, but it does not matter' . . . 'it does matter, but it's too expensive or difficult to do anything about it'.[12]

Long-term vision is also in short supply amongst the masses – according to Rapley, the 'majority of the population is still in disavowal that climate is changing due to human activity'.[13]

Courageous and visionary management of meaning is clearly in short supply too – we simply cannot carry the full burden of causes and effects, but instead deal with them separately and in piece-meal fashion. Even the few who have attempted to articulate highly probable dystopian scenarios stop short of identifying the causes of the apocalypse.

Director Michael Haneke in *The Time of the Wolf*[14] exposes the fragility of civility between a group of strangers thrown together by an undisclosed catastrophe. *The Road* (2006),[15] directed by John Hillcoat based on Cormac McCarthy's[16] almost unbearably disturbing novel, confronts us with yet another undisclosed post-apocalyptic journey by a father and son moving across a desolate, abandoned wasteland of America, pushing a supermarket trolley filled with tattered possessions, most precious among them a gun with two bullets to be fired when the cruelties and hardships encountered on The Road can be endured no more – acceptance that the limit of endurance has been reached being deferred by the father, hour after harrowing hour, for as long as hope lasts.

Both directors engage with the horror of the consequences but not with the cause.

There is a similar pattern of selective engagement with the third future scenario: transformational society. In this hybrid setting of a dystopian utopia, the human species survives through technological fixes and society is transformed by what Monika referred to as morphogenesis or second-order change, and Christensen[17] as a combination of level two disruption (innovation or new markets) and level three disruption (removal of markets altogether). Transformational Society undergoes a major step change (but not before catastrophes threaten extinction) through technological innovation in artificial intelligence, genetic modification and intergalactic travel. Glimpses of such a future are offered by Ridley Scott's iconic *Blade Runner*,[18] set in Los Angeles in 2019(!), and by Michel Houellebecq's novel *The Possibility of an Island*,[19] set in either the last stages of human civilization or at its savage re-birth. Both these works present post-apocalyptic settings without declaring the specific causes of catastrophes.

Only in the fourth scenario for the future, named by Diamond 'the Disciplined Society', do we appear more able to join the dots between causes and consequences.

The Disciplined Society lives within its means by observing the triple bottom line of environmental, social and economic sustainability. The hope offered makes it possible to articulate why change is needed. The real function of utopia is that, unlike dystopia, it allows us to engage with courageous and meaningful management of meaning.

This is the new and most prolific territory of current utopian thinking: the utopia of the Post Carbon Society. It is constructed on the *Hope in the Future for All* and makes an assumption that *The Winner* will not only cease *To Take All* but also that the concept of *The Winner* will be redefined as social values change.

Ideas of the Post Carbon Society are being pursued through policies, research and experimentation across continents, cultures and all disciplines, by individuals, organizations, agencies, cities and nations. All are increasingly networked and share knowledge on how to re-organize the economy and governance, how to retrofit infrastructure and the fabric of cities to optimize use of resources, how to apply new technology to reduce greenhouse gas omissions, to feed the world population, to reduce waste and pollution, to conserve species and resources, and enhance health and wellbeing. The Post Carbon utopia presupposes that the mitigation of and adaptation to environmental challenges are one and the same as mitigation and adaptation of the current greed and unequal consumption.

Utopias failed us in the past maybe for the very reason we are failing now: that we do not learn sufficiently from it – it is myths of the future that have come to drive modern life. 'The self-regulating market was only the latest version of a dream in which the cycles of history have been left behind. If we'd retained some of the constructive paranoia of traditional cultures, we might still not have been able to prevent the neo-liberal experiment; but we would have been better prepared for the fiasco that has ensued.'[20]

It is undisputable that currently we are on the trajectory of 'Business as Usual'. Zygmunt's identified utopias of individual getaway niches cut out from the society and 'once cut out – fenced off tightly, impermeably, from the wilderness doomed to decay' will be short-lived, as Mark Lynas points out in his truly courageous book *Six Degrees*:

> In more densely populated regions, such as Europe or China, isolationist survivalism is simply not an option. Nowhere is properly remote and defensible or offers enough resources for survival. Another option might be stockpiling . . . But defending your supplies from hungry invaders is never easy . . . Hunger is a powerful motivator, and people maddened by hunger or jealousy do not give up. Sooner or later you will run out of ammunition or get caught asleep with your defenses lowered.[21]

The post carbon utopia builds on previous searches for life in balance. If the *Winner Takes All* dystopia prevails, then the closest we will ever get to achieving gardeners' utopias has already passed us by.

The Transformational Society and the Disciplined Society are in the making, and have all the agility and energy that come from having a cause. They should not be underestimated. As we move towards some kind of hybrid of the four scenarios, my hopes and actions are for the Disciplined Society.

This journey need not be painful if shared by all – at

the end of it, we may all wake up to a day of physical comfort, of purpose and conviviality, and with a sense of humility captured by the Swedish phrase *Lagom är bäst* ('The right amount is best').

Monika Kostera   My problem with both utopias – the hunters' as well as the gardeners' – is their obsession with light and their obliviousness of darkness. The original utopia – the Greek Arcadia – was not a place of light and order. It was the kingdom of Pan, the wild god of nature, fertility and theatre. He was lustful and quick to anger, famous for falling in love with nymphs who rejected him, preferring to be turned into trees rather than falling for his charms. Pan was also a great musician and admirer of beauty, and his Arcadia was indeed a beautiful – but far from one-sided or linear – place. The idea of seeing in it an earthly paradise, a place of utopian peace, derives from the Renaissance, from its dreams of pure nature, unpolluted by humanity and civilization. Yet, even then, artists, such as Nicolas Poussin or Guercino, knew that it had to contain a profound darkness and mystery. Poussin's painting *Et in Arcadia ego* depicts an idyllic scene of shepherds convening in a spot of ethereal and numinous beauty. Yet the central point in the image is occupied by a huge, shadowy tomb. One of the men is tracing letters inscribed in it, and his finger encounters his own shadow, twisted in a contemplative position, as if touching his shadowy head. Guercino's Arcadia is even darker: the beauty of the landscape consists in its very darkness, and the indeterminacy, the vagueness of the scene (are the two men in the picture terrified or in awe; sad or happy; is the skull frightening or beautiful? – perhaps both?) is precisely what makes the image so powerful. The sky and the characters are shadowy and at the same time illuminated by a fervent light, transcending the background, and at the same time letting itself be consumed by it. These are my favourite images of Arcadia and of utopia – a place where darkness and light meet, where they each tell their own story, as in everyday reality, but also work together to tell a more powerful, all-encompassing tale together, which has the power to go beyond time and to awaken imagination. My utopia, like Guercino's Arcadia, is not a harmonious and ordered place, motivating the inhabitants to undertake activities of thrift, resourcefulness or entrepreneurship. It compels the human being to look for answers beyond its frame, perhaps in history, art, literature – to find inspiration in feelings and dreams.

At least since the Enlightenment, but especially in the era which you, Zygmunt, call solid modernity, humanity – and in particular the West – has been obsessed by figures of light. The history of progress, be it scientific, social or technological, unfolds like one of Fra Angelico's canvases – scenes suffused with light, with shadows so frail and weedy that they almost surrender to the radiance. In some of his paintings, the figures cast no shadows at all. In contemporary times Western civilization has reached such a shadowless apogee: mystery has been banned from our speech, our hopes, our imagination; there is no language and no place for talking about things that are not perfectly rational, linear, preferably numeric. In our own profession it is no longer considered desirable to write books, and academic articles have become relentlessly linear. Leading journals no longer publish anything that lacks a clear structure and – God forbid – unfolds in a surprising way. They did, until quite recently, as a matter of exception; nowadays only the most famous authors can see their less than strictly rigid texts appear in print. In media, even in everyday talk, we are supposed to express ourselves in a clear and logical fashion, always say that we are happy – always feel happy – be optimistic, fight against dark thoughts and illness, marginalize the uncertain, belittle the unknown, always act in extroverted ways and as if we were to live forever within our current material frames. For doubts, sadness, even for sudden flights of enthusiasm and fancy, we are to take drugs – the complex modern equivalent of bromide. At all costs, we are to remain calm, balanced and pursue 'wellness',[22] the perfect decision makers to fit into the neo-liberal creed of incessantly making the correct and rational choices. Even of love, death – even of our dreams – we are now to talk only in rational terms – if possible, financial ones.

Until recently the East used to be the guardian of darkness. I mean the East farther away geographically, but also Eastern Europe, the home of Chekhov, Dostoyevsky, Kieślowski, Cioran, of plaintive poetry, ominous prophecies, and disturbing philosophy. Eastern Europe used to be the keeper of the unknown, of mystery and sorrow, through its culture of intellectuals – like yourself, Zygmunt – defying classification and ordering, holders of enormous intellectual courage and of genuine talent, to write in a way that inspires masses of readers but where it is exceedingly difficult to find 'the contribution' and which flows without a 'clear structure'. The neo-liberal revolution of the late 1980s and the early 1990s compelled the East to imitate the West, to try to become even more 'Western' than their neighbours and to renounce, loudly – maybe even more vigorously than the West itself – everything that was not strictly linear or lying within the domain of perfect light. The Utopia we have been so busy building since then is, to me, a blinding kind of dystopia, maybe destined for the likes of Fra Angelico's characters – angels and saints – but definitely not meant for human eyes. Suffused with a light that is so omni-present, intrusive and disturbing that it, in fact, kills. The West, longing for darkness, seeks it out in a variety of substitutes, of which sarcasm and the cult of irony are perhaps the most popular among intellectuals. And yet they are but a meagre and unfulfilling replacement: they allow the writer and the speaker to flirt with darkness, to caress it, embrace it for a moment – but then it compels him or her to forcefully reject it, renounce and repudiate it. He or she is left, once again, in the spotlight. This course is as unsustainable for thought and imagination as relentless devastation and pollution are for the natural environment. This is the end. And yet, as in all of human history, it is not. We, humanity, do not have to walk into the wall; we can look for new ways that will lead us out of the mess we are in and that, perhaps, will be more interesting, more full of life than the current dead-end street.

So, my invitation is this: let's come together, East and West, darkness and light, bring forward what is left of the darkness in the East, for it is still there – ready to be shared with the West. The West has been complaining about the unbalanced character of the relationship with what they label 'new Europe' and yet their mistake is in this precisely – Eastern Europe is not new, it is only pretending to be so. And yes, the West has not been taking anything of much value from the East recently; it is time the West started taking, started learning, from the East. It is time we, Easterners, shared what we still have in abundance – the darkness. Let's together leave Fra Angelico's domain of immaculate light to angels and saints, while we, human beings, consider, once again, the heritage of Arcadia. And we will have to use whatever is there, for it has been changed during the centuries of civilization and progress. It is now full of cities, technology, scientific discoveries, art, culture and, yes, management models. In my Utopia – to which, I guess, my book *Occupy Management!*[23] is dedicated – these things are radically recycled, re-used, re-claimed – not necessarily in a productive way, but just because they are there. Modernity, like a giant waste heap in Arcadia, has to be salvaged and reprocessed or else it will rot and kill all life on this planet with its poisonous miasma.

ZB Utopias and dystopias have one prominent thing in common: namely, adumbration of an end to change, assumed to be irreversible; postulating a point to which all things could/would eventually arrive only to bring to a halt all further movement and stay still – until the evidently un-human Nature, no longer in need of human interference and resentful of it for its being as uncouth and unkempt as much as obtrusive and obtuse, takes its course. Leon Battista Alberti[24] portrayed the state of perfection: a state in which all and any further change may be only for the worse (read: shorter of its ideal condition), rendering the state of affairs less good and agreeable in the case of utopias, or less evil and disagreeable in the case of dystopias. Utopias and dystopias portray ends to the road, but for that reason also immobility, standstill and infinite stagnation, which no one – or almost no one – has a wish and a resolve to break – while a few solitary rebels, like Winston Smith in Orwell's *1984*[25] or Bernard Marx and John the Savage of Huxley's *Brave New World*,[26] are doomed to be crushed whenever they try to challenge the status quo.

Utopias and dystopias alike, though for opposing reasons, adumbrate an end to the hubbub and bustle marking the choices comprising human existence: the first because change is no longer desirable; the second because change is no longer possible. There is a difference inside the similarity: utopia shows in what way the current state of affairs may be changed and so its slide into perdition averted, whereas dystopia calculates the consequences of neglecting that advice. Utopia is (can be, is meant to be) a call to arms, whereas dystopia proclaims the obsoleteness and uselessness of arms should the neglect last long enough to reach the point of no return; utopia nudges its audience to pursue the dream of (far-away, ultimate) tranquillity that would follow prompt and successful surgery on a diseased society, whereas dystopia adumbrates the horrors of quietism resulting from surgery postponed or abandoned. Utopians want their visions to act as self-fulfilling prophecies. Dystopians, on the other hand, want – as did the prophets of the Hebrew Bible – their visions to be prevented from coming true. Both are indispensable – both are needed. Between them, they allow us to glimpse the difference between the roads we should take and those we are warned to avoid. The siren songs of either can be listened to; alternatively, one can also follow Odysseus' example, tying one's own legs and hands to the mast and plugging the ears of the ship's crew: a ploy to which, as Irena rightly suggests, we are all too often prompted to resort – or to which we find ourselves abandoned for lack of other realistic strategies. It is not, however, the alternative between pricking up one's ears and plugging them that stands behind the success or failure of the utopian–dystopian tandems. As Marx warned long ago, and (as Monika reminds us) both Guercino and Poussin vividly depicted in their versions of *Et in Arcadia Ego*, people make history, though not under conditions of their own choosing.

I admit that I fully share Irena's sympathy for the utopian model of 'disciplined' or 'post-carbon' society, which is not just the best conceivable prospect for the 'mitigation of and adaptation to environmental changes', but, given the depth and consequentiality of those changes, a matter of no less than life or death – certainly for humans, but possibly for life as such. However, I also share Monika's attraction to an Arcadia that, in her own words, 'is not a harmonious and ordered place, motivating the inhabitants to undertake activities of thrift, resourcefulness or entrepreneurship' and, let me add, ubiquitous and omnivorous management – in other words, attraction to what has been left in Arcadia of the spirit of Pan. And that spirit, in a nutshell, is marked by endemic under-determination and under-definition; creatures animated by it wouldn't sacrifice their capability of self-reinvention and self-reassertion on the altar of freedom from risk and from the possibility of error promised by the light and transparency obsessively worshipped and compulsively celebrated in the 'project of modernity', which did its best to deliver on that promise (even if, fortunately for us all, the 'best' that it was doing in pursuit of the implied or proclaimed goal proved to be not up to the daunting task it set for itself).

The big question, in my mind, is how to reconcile the two utopias: which layers of our current condition do we need to dig up, re-examine and recycle in order to render such a reconciliation plausible, or even feasible? And so I ask myself: what is hidden/incarcerated/embalmed inside Poussin's giant coffin? Or whose skull baffled the two very much alive, albeit also much worried, spectators (newcomers to Arcadia?) on Guercino's canvas?

5

Craftsmanship

Jerzy Kociatkiewicz   I would like us, if possible, to continue the utopian strand of our conversation until the weight of the issues facing us combines to send us crashing back to the *terra firma* of more earthly concerns. But I would also like to introduce to our utopian vocabulary the notion of heterotopia, originally coined in 1967 by Michel Foucault in his essay 'Of Other Spaces: Utopias and Heterotopias'. For Foucault, the term denoted an actual space (as opposed to an imagined one) laced with multiple contradictory meanings, representing a form of challenge to the self-consistency of the dominant discursive order. Given how complex and self-contradictory any social system is bound to be, 'there is probably not a single culture in the world that is not made up of heterotopias'.[1]

But when the term was picked up by Samuel Delany in his science fiction novel *Trouble on Triton: An Ambiguous Heterotopia*,[2] it was taken to mean an imagined society that simultaneously reflected the desires of the author and transcended the utopia/dystopia divide, but also a society that did not follow a single hegemonic organizational template. Utopias, representing the best possible social arrangement, have a tendency of assuming a single universal solution (though it should be noted that Huxley's dystopian *Brave New World* included the rigidly structured main cities, the lax but insignificant research centres in the margins, and a reservation for the yet uncivilized). And yet the utopian meetings of light and darkness postulated by Monika are possible only insofar as, following God's very first biblical gesture, the light and the darkness remain separate.

In the early years of this century, Richard Florida[3] prophesized the ascendance of what he termed 'the creative class': artists, technology workers and bohemians whose ability to transform their lived surroundings for themselves as well as for others was to make them the powerhouse of future economic and, particularly, urban development.

Ten years later, we can more clearly appreciate both the astuteness and the naïveté of Florida's expectations. Just by looking outside my window I can attest to the amount of pleasure that street murals, largely unlicensed and painted by the endlessly creative Sheffield street artists, bring into the life of my neighbourhood, though whether they bring any economic benefits to the city is a much more contentious proposition. What is quite obvious, though, is that street artists, professionals in creative industries, and technology workers share little in the benefits from the rise in value of neighbourhoods gentrified, in part at least, through their activities. A recent and widely re-posted discussion on the (web)pages of the *Telegraph*[4] highlighted both the contribution and the precariousness of the position of the cultural worker understood as urban regenerator.

We can, of course, hope that the generative class of the future will be able to avoid these pitfalls: after all, wild hopes are the bedrock of utopian thinking. And it is here that I would like to bring up a figure I see as interesting for all our utopian sensibilities: the crafts-man as envisaged by Richard Sennett.[5] This notion of a craftsperson combines the long history of craft-focused work organization with the possibility of finding one's work meaningful, worthwhile, and rewarding in itself. It appears as an attractive alternative to modern (solid or liquid) forms of work, and has served as an inspi-ration for numerous attempts to relieve workplace alienation, starting with William Morris's Arts and Crafts movement in the mid nineteenth century.

The part of Sennett's exploration that I find particu-larly engrossing is his examination of the links between craftsmanship and obsession: acquiring craftsmanship requires dedication, and excellence demands levels of dedication that not only threaten any notion of work–life balance, but also require treating work as a goal rather than a means to an end, business-driven or oth-erwise. Sennett also recalls W. Edwards Deming's work on what came to be called Total Quality Management (TQM): the refocusing of effort throughout the entire organization on continual improvement of the quality of its output. This was indeed a total proposition: quality was to become the obsessive goal and the responsibil-ity of each member of the organization, overriding all other considerations. The idea's original application within Japanese industry has often been cited as one of the reasons for its successes throughout the 1960s and

1970s. As a result, TQM came to be treated, both by its proponents and by its critics, as a tool for building financial success or market dominance of the company adopting its tenets, but such reformulation is invariably self-defeating: obsession cannot be contained as just one tool in the management toolkit. Robbed of its dangerous edge (for a failure to consider anything but product quality is certainly dangerous), the obsession becomes an unconvincing platitude (and there are many of these indeed in the management toolkits of our times).

You, Zygmunt, once described yourself as a 'craftsman of sociological prose',[6] opposing craftsmanship to poetry. The remark seems to build on C. Wright Mills's ideal of sociology as intellectual craftsmanship;[7] his craftsman stood in opposition to the box-ticking bureaucrat of mechanized sociology.[8] Monika, your current research looks at small, sustainable enterprises which appear to be perfect places to foster both expertise and personal obsessions. And you, Irena, come from a profession that has perhaps the strongest claim to maintaining traditions of craftsmanship – 'It can be said that at the heart of architecture is the idea that we, as architects and designers, are really craftsmen', wrote Edward Kundla in an American Institute of Architects report on craftsmanship.[9]

It is, then, possible, that the figure of the craftsman, or a craftsperson, will be intimately familiar to all of us, and, so, I would like to ask about how you see the place of craftsmanship both in the liquid modern present and in the utopian/dystopian societies you have sketched in the previous chapter.

Monika Kostera Heterotopias are, as you say, Jerzy, radically different places. Michel Foucault envisages

93

them as 'real places, actual places, places that are designed into the very institution of society, which are sorts of actually realized utopias in which the real emplacements ... are, at the same time, represented, contested, and reversed'.[10] You ask how art, craftsmanship and organizing may come together and what the encounter may bring. Daniel Hjorth[11] describes just such a project, initiated by the Danish artist Kent Hansen, aimed at bringing business and art closer together. In this project, artists cooperated with employees from different enterprises to create better work-spaces. Ultimately, they hoped for a renewal of workplaces, giving a free rein to creativity and making work a better experience. Hjorth observed one of the sites where this project was very successfully introduced and noticed that it was not so-called 'high' art, a groundbreaking and sublime creative expression, but more mundane, shop-floor-level art that really took root and transformed the experience of people working in the place concerned by the introduction of small but very effective heterotopias, on the margins of both 'high art' and 'real business'. Artists from the group Superflex developed, together with the workers, a place for play, or, indeed, somewhere they could do whatever they pleased, located in a small container supported by metal frames, raised above the floor level. The workers' wish was to build a 'haven for their own time'. One of the employees said: 'Here, at the end of the project, my expectations have moved in another direction. I believe that this and similar projects in the days to come can break down harming monotony or sameness and inspire to new ideas about what a workday might look like, to the benefit and enjoyment for the labor market of the future.'[12] The container was equipped with whiteboards, computers and hosted a local radio station, where the employees could broadcast to the whole company. In such a place out of place, time out of time, the employees were free from the managerially organized rhythms and could create rhythms of their own. They could also do nothing at all, but, as it turns out, they preferred to use the freedom in active ways. Daniel Hjorth suggests that in this case 'art becomes liberated as art; ideas of what could be actualized are related to desire and power.'[13]

As you say, Jerzy, I am now living in Sheffield, in an area alive with street-art, with artwork by artists known world-wide, such as Rocketo1, Phlegm or Kid Acne, and others, not preserved as in a gallery or museum, but constantly shifting, changing, with new images appearing once in a while, and with a never-ending stream of visitors, with or without notebooks and cameras, visible every day. The artwork is there free to see and enjoy for anyone who comes this way – some of it monumental, like Rocketo1's giant fresco of Charles Darwin, some of it modestly fitted into the nooks and spaces of the crumbling industrial architecture, like Kid Acne's smiling cigarette. The delicious liminality of the space, together with a sense of it being completely and radically different from the city centre, just two streets and perhaps three minutes' walk away, makes it a perfect heterotopia, a space out of space, time out of time. Here art tends to happen and people tend to engage with it. As an observer of and dweller in the space – we live in an old building right in the middle of it all – I am constantly aware of its attraction and energy, like the call of the sirens; not only am I curious to see each day whether anything new has appeared on the walls, but my own senses are somehow sharpened and my mind compelled to spin perhaps more than usual, and not necessarily around topics related to organization theory. And yet I think of organizing very often as I pass by here, of how natural and spontaneous it can be, how much of a vital need it is for people, and how disorderly and anarchic it can get. This space is quite remarkably organized in its own way, if decidedly not in a mainstream understanding of the word. Like a centre of gravity, it attracts people, ideas, visions and meanings, and produces collages that, like in a kaleidoscope, shift every day. One day I notice certain elements; the next, others stick out more, even without new elements being added. The space produces its own ephemeral synergies of images, light, aura and looking.

You mention, Jerzy, the small ecofirms I currently study,[14] as an example of heterotopias of craftsmanship. I agree that these organizations also are, like the street-art in Sheffield, spaces out of space and times out of time, where organizing happens on its own terms and is a natural drive rather than a managerial tool for making people, things and happenings fit into a scheme of effectivity and profitability. These small organizations often proudly emphasize that they are not businesses but ways of life, activities making it possible for the organizers to make a difference, or express themselves artistically. In most of these firms art plays a role, but it is usually a street-level or shop-floor-level art, such as fantastic cakes created by the owners of a vegan restaurant, rooms dedicated to heroes and heroines of the cooperative movement designed by the owners of a hostel, or the wild creations of children and the personnel in a kindergarten. Good craftsmanship is the most cherished value in all these firms, expressed in their day-to-day work, products and services offered to their clients, and also in the pride and often joy the people take in fixing their own problems, making repairs themselves (instead of calling an outside service), sharing the responsibility of cleaning the spaces (instead of employing a cleaner), and so on. Art and craftsmanship make their work-experience whole, I believe, and reunite the process of production, which modernity has divided and splintered, from the introduction of the assembly line and so called 'scientific management'.[15] Power and freedom to define the work process was taken away from workers and office employees, the disenfranchisement reaching higher and higher administrative levels.[16] In the end, even managers were subjected to routines of rationalization, specialization and standardization of their work. Factories became giant machines, and the workers were seen as mere fallible additions to the conveyor belt. Offices soon followed on the same path, turning into monstrous administrative machines. This is what most of the corporate and mainstream public-sector work looks like today – something that the small firms that I study have managed to turn away from and disregard. I think that they succeed in doing this thanks to the active cultivation of their status as heterotopias, organizations that do not need to follow the major trends or even know what they are, people who never ask themselves at meetings what the 'fat cats' are doing outside – and frankly they do not care. They define themselves, instead, as 'doing their own thing', which they easily can relate to – it is strongly demarcated by their values and ideas, such as ecology, diversity or creativity. Art and craft are very often actively used as a source of inspiration, producing the energy needed to run the organization on a day-to-day basis, as well as a signature of the individuality and uniqueness of the organization.

I am curious: what reflections on and experiences of the role of art and craft in the creation and management of heterotopias do you have, Zygmunt and Irena? Do you see them as I do, as sources of organizational energy and individuation in the fields that interest you: society and the city?

Zygmunt Bauman Heterotopia ... The idea of it, the attempts to embody the idea, and the retrospective baptizing of those trials as heterotopia (the space 'out there'), were the unplanned offspring of the dystopia that managed to stifle utopian hopes like those of William Morris, recalled by Jerzy – or, for that matter, of Henry David Thoreau or Thorstein Veblen. Choosing the name 'heterotopia' for the diffuse and scattered attempts to salvage whatever was left of those hopes signalled surrender – whether by design or by default. In the last account, 'heteronomia' means: in this world there is no room for utopian dreams. Exile – that, to repeat after Monika, 'place out of place, time out of time', that 'haven for their own work' – is the utopias' only imaginable habitat, or the last dug-out for whatever remained of their relics; heterotopia, I am tempted to say, is on the other hand a utopia of a shelter or a hiding place from the 'real world', not a project of a world organized and managed differently from the world as it is.

The problem that we try to address in putting our heads together is whether such a world, differently managed and organized, is conceivable; and if it is conceivable, then where are we to start and how are we to go about lifting what in the present world is a 'place out of place, time out of time' to the status of a 'full place' and a 'complete time'? Is a world managed and organized differently from the world we inhabit – a world hell-bent on growth of individualization, consumerism, waste and social inequality – conceivable? This is the question that Jeremy Rifkin, in his latest oeuvre under the unduly baffling title *The Zero Marginal Cost Society*, and subtitled *The Internet of Things, The Collaborative Commons, and the Eclipse of Capitalism*,[17] confronts point blank. The answers Rifkin offers – answers grounded in a uniquely thorough research of an astonishingly large volume of facts – are astoundingly radical and constitute a powerful challenge to the prevailing (Antonio Gramsci[18] would say 'hegemonic') creed of our times, expressed and embraced from the top to bottom of society – from the philosophy of the learned classes down to the common sense of the hoi polloi. What Rifkin argues is that an alternative to capitalist markets, widely viewed as an eternal feature of human nature, is not just conceivable, but already born and gaining ground – and is likely to become dominant not in a matter of centuries, but a few decades.

To put Rifkin's thesis in a nutshell: capitalism is on the way out, gradually yet unstoppably and irreversibly replaced by 'collaborative commons', which is apparently new, though deeply rooted in the pre-capitalist histori-cal mode of human cohabitation. Commons predate, as Rifkin reminds us, the modern/capitalist institutions and are in fact 'the oldest form of institutionalised, self-managed activity in the world'.[19] And he explains in the shortest possible way how the starting point and the destination of the current transformation differ: 'While the capitalist market is based on self-interest and driven by material gain, the social Commons is motivated by collaborative interests and driven by a deep desire to connect with others and share. If the former promotes property rights, caveat emptor, and the search for autonomy, the latter advances open-source innovation, transparency, and the search for community.'[20] When he refers to the capitalism he considers to be currently on the wane, Rifkin means 'a unique and peculiar form of enterprise in which the workforce is stripped of its ownership of the tools it uses to create the products, and the investors who own the enterprises are stripped of their power to control and manage their businesses'.[21] In contrast, the 'Collaborative Commons', Rifkin insists, are not a utopian Fairyland of never-never, but a reality around the next corner – a reality separated from the present condition not by a revolution, world war or other catastrophe, but by the 'exponentially shrinking' stretch of time needed for the maturation of already planted, budding and flowering forms of togetherness and modes of communication, procuring energy and resolving logistical problems. Once fully mature, collaborative commons will 'break the monopoly hold of giant, vertically integrated companies operating in capitalist markets by enabling peer production in laterally scaled continental and global networks at near zero marginal cost'.[22]

Rifkin argues throughout his study that just as the steam engine enabled/prompted/necessitated the first industrial revolution, and as the internal combustion engine together with the telephone network set in motion the second industrial revolution, the currently emerging global 'Internet of Things', integrating the communications Internet with the energy Internet and logistics (mobility) Internet, will supply the infrastructure for the third industrial revolution. He also points out[23] that although the idea of such integration and the term 'Internet of Things' were coined already in 1995, they stayed for quite a few years on a side burner due to the high cost of implanting sensors and actuators required for remote monitoring and control, and the limited capacity of an Internet that allowed only 4.5 billion unique addresses. With 'radio-frequency identification chips' now available for less than 10 cents each, and a new Internet protocol allowing 340 trillion trillion trillion addresses, those barriers have been swept out of the way – and the word is about to be made flesh . . . With marginal costs of communication and energy coming down close to zero (Internet communication is already practically free, whereas we don't pay the Sun, wind or ocean waves for the energy they supply and we capture), and with universally available 3D printing that by-passes the commercial markets on the (rapid) rise, the ground available for an economy led by greed for material gain is rapidly shrinking and getting scarce. The historical episode of such an economy is grinding to a halt. The era of cooperation and sharing is about to start.

In the coming era, both capitalism and socialism will lose their once-dominant hold over society, as a new generation increasingly identifies with Collaboratism.[24] To many – perhaps most – of us, such a prediction smacks of pure idle fantasy – as did visions of the textile giants of Manchester, not to mention Ford or GM-style factories, to the creators of miniature cottage-sized enterprises. One should, however, derive from these – and numerous other similar – historical cases the advice to abstain prudently from dismissing Rifkin's prognosis light-heartedly. When browsing many years ago through the pages of the nineteenth-century *Manchester Guardian*, a daily published in the very heart of the ongoing industrial revolution, I was astonished to find out that, despite the plethora of news about new factories popping up all around the city like mushrooms after rain, there were virtually no signs of awareness that what all those scattered bits of information amounted to was nothing less than an economic, social and cultural revolution. The summary label of 'industrial revolution' was stamped on all that only retrospectively.

As a matter of fact, Rifkin prods us to scan the present-day global landscape in its totality, rather than watching on screens or newspaper pages its diffuse, scattered, kaleidoscopic and variegated fragments; and – unlike our nineteenth-century ancestors – to spot thereby the forest behind the trees, rather than waiting for the benefit of hindsight to integrate the scattered pictures into a meaningful whole. Rifkin suggests that the 'contemporary Commons' can be seen already. They are composed by 'billions of people who engage in the deeply social aspects of life'. They are 'made up of literally millions of self-managed, mostly democratically run organizations, including charities, religious bodies, arts and cultural groups, educational foundations, amateur sports clubs, producer and consumer cooperatives, credit unions, health-care organizations, advocacy groups, condominium associations, and a near endless list of other formal and informal institutions that generate the social capital of society'.[25] Social capital is there and growing, waiting to be harvested, garnered, set to work.

Rifkin is right when he calls for us to rip down the curtain hung by the market-run consumerist society before increasingly tangible and realistic possibilities of alternatives to itself – of a society of *collaboration* instead of *competition*. But it is one thing to ask us – rightly – to resist the temptation to neglect or dismiss what are still just sprouts of commons-style social settings (all majorities have to begin from a tiny minority, and the most branchy of oak trees originated from tiny acorns) – and quite another to make the doubtful suggestion that the case is already open and shut and the outcome of the current transformation is predetermined. This smacks of a new version of 'technological determinism'. But axes can be equally easily used to chop wood or heads – and while technology determines the set of options open to humans, it does not determine which of the options will be eventually taken and which suppressed. The track of technological development is not a one-way street, and even less is it a street pre-designed and laid out in advance of its construction. Rifkin presents, however, the collaborative commons as the sole scenario, the certainty of its implementation being already assured courtesy of the logic of technology. What humans *can* do is perhaps a question that can and should be addressed to technology. What humans *will* do, however, is a question better addressed to politics, sociology, psychology – with the ultimate answers unlikely to be given other than with the benefit of hindsight.

Similarly debatable is the decision to assign the status of the 'infrastructure' determining the 'collaborative commons' character of the society-to-come to computer technology. Universal, easy and convenient exposure to world events in 'real time', coupled with opening similarly universal, and equally easy, undisturbed entry to the public stage, has been already welcomed by numerous observers as a genuine turning point in the brief, though eventful and stormy, history of modern democracy. Contrary to quite widespread expectations that the Internet would be a great step forward in the history of democracy, involving all of us in shaping the world that we share and replacing the inherited 'pyramid of power' with a 'lateral' politics, evidence accumulates, however, that the Internet may also serve to perpetuate and reinforce conflicts and antagonisms, while preventing an effective polylogue that might carry a chance of armistice and eventual agreement – integration and mutually beneficial collaboration. Paradoxically, the danger arises from the inclination of most internauts to make the online world a conflict-free zone – though not by negotiating the conflict-generating issues, and resolving these conflicts to mutual satisfaction, but thanks to the removal from sight and mind of the conflicts haunting the offline world.

Numerous studies have shown that Internet-dedicated users can and do spend great parts (perhaps most) of their time or even their whole online life encountering solely like-minded people. The Internet creates an improved version of a 'gated community': unlike its offline equivalent it does not charge the occupiers an exorbitant rent and does not need armed guards or a sophisticated CCTV network – a simple 'delete' key will suffice. The attraction of all and any – online as offline – gated communities is that one lives there in the company of strictly pre-selected people, 'people like you', like-minded people – free from the intrusion of strangers whose presence might require awkward negotiation of a mode of cohabitation and present a challenge to your self-assurance that your mode of life is the only proper one, bound to be shared by everybody within your sight and reach. They are mirrored reflections of yourself and you are a mirror reflecting them, therefore by living there you are not taking the risk of falling out with your neighbour, of arguing or fighting about political, ideological or indeed any other kind of issues. A comfort zone indeed, sound-insulated from the hubbub of diversified and variegated, quarrelsome crowds roaming the city streets and workplaces. The only snag is that, in such an artificially yet artfully disinfected, sanitized online environment, one can hardly develop immunity to the toxins of controversy endemic to the offline universe, or learn the art of stripping them of their morbid and eventually murderous potential. And because one has failed to learn it, the divisions and contentions carried by strangers in city streets appear even more threatening – and perhaps incurable. Divisions born online are equipped with a self-propelling and self-exacerbating capacity.

Irena Bauman   Like strangers arriving in a new city, I am in the habit of recklessly roaming through the unfamiliar territory, navigating only by intuition. Inevitably, following several returns to the same crossroad, many frustrating dead ends, and numerous failures to get closer to the desired destination, I finally capitulate and turn to the signposts for guidance.

The conversation on the role of craftsmanship lends itself to similar roaming: I know intuitively that craftsmanship sits at the heart of all that we are collectively exploring – the themes of interregnum, of redistribution, of utopias, heterotopias, of wellbeing, of changing management structures and of collaborative commons – but not all alleyways will lead to the single space of clarity. The critical question here is not so much Zygmunt's of whether we can or will choose the route that is the right one, but more: Which one of the many routes *is* the right one?

To avoid the risk of unproductive roaming, I have chosen two signposts at different starting points, in the hope that these will lead to a single point of convergence: the stories of Santiago Bell and of Bill Strickland are one, and the 'Making Revolution' is the other. Santiago Bell, a Chilean exile, arrived at the door of the United Reformed Church in Bromley-by-Bow in the east end of London, one Tuesday afternoon in 1985.

Andrew Mawson, then the Christian Minister (now Baron Mawson, OBE), described how: 'The man I saw when I opened the door that day with his weathered face and wise eyes, had manifestly been through a terrible ordeal . . . he was looking for somewhere to rebuild his life. Everything in my being told me that that place was right here, with me in Bromley-by-Bow.'[26] He offered Santiago all he had, which was a small derelict room in the church. Andrew Mawson goes on to describe how Santiago began to arrive each day with pieces of timber he had scavenged from local skips:

> He soon cleared the room, painted the walls white, brought in a few personal tools and began to build – or, more accurately, sculpt – a workbench. The joints were so close fitting, and it was all so expertly made, that it could have taken the weight of an elephant. This was no ordinary joiner and we knew it. The word soon got around.[27]

Santiago and Andrew went on to build both a community of people and a physical place: Bromley-by-Bow Centre, an internationally acclaimed community centre, a laboratory for social innovation and enterprise. Today it offers over 100 events per week, an impressive range of social enterprises in art, health, education and practical skills, to one of the most deprived communities in London. Andrew acknowledges the role that Santiago played in this achievement: he also knew and understood how to build a community. He knew that real change must be built of something solid, built timber by timber, relationship by relationship.[28]

Bromley-by-Bow Centre is not another tacky, run-down municipal building. It is aspirational and made with high-quality furnishings and innovative design, a declaration of entrepreneurship and community pride.

Across the Atlantic, in Pittsburgh, Bill Strickland, the President of Manchester Bidwell Corporation tells another story of how, as a young black kid about to flunk out of school, he walked past a ceramist's studio and happened to look in: 'here was this man throwing pots. Frank Ross. Now then I don't know how many of you have ever seen a ceramics wheel turning, but if you have you know its magic. It was like a big invisible hand lifted me to that wheel. Mr Ross looked up and said: "can I help you?"'[29] From this relationship, formed 'around a revolving mound of clay', the Manchester Craftsman Guild evolved, for which Strickland raised grants whilst still in college. It started life as an after-school arts programme for kids from the ghetto and now, each year, it serves some 3,900 young people from disadvantaged backgrounds, with classes in various crafts including ceramics, jazz, catering, graphics and art. Many of them go on to higher education, and there are now twenty more guilds such as this one rolled out across America.

Bill Strickland insists that the process of making and quality and beauty have the power to enable young people to achieve the impossible – to overcome the disadvantages they were born into and to make something of their lives. Just as in Bromley-by-Bow Centre, the Manchester Craftsman Guild is furnished with handmade crafted furniture. Every week fresh orchids are bought for the entrance hall.

Neither Andrew nor Bill are makers in the conventional sense, but their own form of drive towards a concept of excellence found a natural partnership in the values that underpin the work of accomplished craftsmen such as Santiago and Ross. All four men shared the desire to make something that lasts and is of value in its own right, and all four pursued the notions of excellence with the obsessive tenacity that Jerzy has already noted. It is the same tenacity with which Jean-Baptist Grenouille, the perfumer, pursued the scent of Laura across eighteenth-century France so that he could harvest the essence to make the most exquisite of all perfumes ever made;[30] the same obsession with which the fifteenth-century Russian bell maker Boriska relentlessly searched for the right clay from which to make the casting mould whilst hundreds of workman stood by for weeks impatiently waiting.[31] And the same obsession drove Babette Harsan, a French refugee sheltering in a nineteenth-century Danish village, to spend a small fortune won in a lottery on crafting a single dinner, fit for nobility but consumed by a handful of un-worldly and suspicious villagers, so that she could practice her culinary skills just one more time.[32]

Since the times in which these craftsmen obsessed over their respective crafts, the industrial revolution has severed the ropes that tethered consumption to the processes and the understanding of production. And ever since, like a pea under twenty mattresses causing discomfort to a princess,[33] the loss of creative skills – one of the strongest of human impulses and one of the most significant means of human expression – leaves a constant, barely articulated ache in our lives of consumption.

We manage this ache either through treatment of the symptoms or, increasingly, through preventative action. The 'treatment' takes the form of values we attach to craftsmanship: the distinction between junk and antiques, between second-hand and vintage, and between the decision to demolish or to list a building. The ache is bearable as long as we can see that not all is lost.

We take preventative action when we turn to making once again. Our aversion to consumerism and its staple diet of 'Total Works of Commerce' – those surplus-to-requirement items that, in the words of Bruce Sterling, 'enter our lives through brand management, the purchase experience and the ritual un-boxing'[34] – is quietly growing. The economic crises, the hollowing-out of the job market and the longing for a more sustainable way of living have created a delicious cocktail of necessity and desire.

These examples bring me to a new exploration and a new signpost: the Making Revolution. The conversion of social values from 'consuming' into 'prosuming', originally foreseen and named by Alvin Toffler as far back as 1970,[35] is now underway, generating new forms of making, new types of craftsmen and a new infrastructure of institutions and of management tools to support them – the world of the Internet of Things, and the rise of the collaborative commons already brought into our conversation by Zygmunt.

New institutions such as FabLabs, initiated by Massachusetts Institute of Technology in 2001, now available in over 100 cities worldwide, are physical places for the Making Revolution. They provide facilities for digital making, peer-to-peer project-based technical training, problem-solving, small-scale high-tech business incubation and grassroots research.

Neil Gershenfeld, the creator of the FabLab network, recounts how, after the first lab opened in Boston:

> there was then a strong link to a community in Ghana, which led to a Lab going there. Then there was a strong link to South Africa. And every time we opened a lab there are suddenly 10 more. But it's not OUR plan. People need these in their communities – for a range of reasons. Nobody is pushing and there isn't a formal process. People pull, and that's how it spreads.[36]

FabLabs are the institutions of the collaborative commons enabling direct contact between makers, designers and users, and the integration of production and distribution: 'designs can be made anywhere in the world. They can be made locally, or they can be designed locally and made anywhere';[37] 'It is the data that is shipped not the product. FabLabs encourage people to work in an open way because the infringement is so easy that there is no way to ensure ownership. Sharing isn't imposed ... it's an operational consequence.'[38] Sharing and collaboration are also the principles of the grassroots-led Hackerspace – an international network of open community labs with tools where hackers can come together to share resources and knowledge to make and build things.

New forms of sharing, Makers Fairs in metropolitan cities, and their counterparts Mini Maker Fairs in smaller cities, are popping up across the world and are attended to capacity wherever they take place, affirming Bruce Sterling's suggestion that 'Dad's urge to tinker and Mum's keenness to knit are in no more danger than Mum and Dad themselves.'[39]

And Mum and Dad are not doing it alone – Social Making is rife: skill-share events in sewing are taking place in cafés in many cities, round-robin quilts are made through international networks of patch-workers. Hackers build their own tools and are 'mashing' software to fit their own needs. These activities are sustained through online social networks and events such as the Stitch 'n Bitch[40] knitting groups (4,603 of them established in 289 locations across the world), and the 3rd Revolution Sewing Network that calls for: 'crafters, makers, artists, do-it-yourself-ers, and hobbyists' to UNITE![41]

Bruce Sterling suggests that consumerism is being inverted and repurposed. Just-in-time factory processes, until recently only available to multinationals, are now available to all makers, who are free to browse the international market for any part they require; commercial interests protected by complex processes involving patents and copyrights are rendered redundant by free software that unites new production networks; corporate contracts and joint ventures are bypassed with Application Programming Interfaces (API), which is allowing cheap and hobbyist software to interface directly with expensive professional software now commonly exploited in Mashups (in my own practice the Mashup of Grasshopper – cheap hobbyist software – and Rhino – expensive professional software – is allowing us to investigate the possibility of creating mass bespoke home designs). Small makers can access international markets through websites such as Etsy, which retails handmade products directly from makers.

The peer-to-peer markets that reduce friction and lower barriers to entry are enabling millions to open their own micro-sized making businesses and the artisan market has exploded onto the scene. The 3rd Industrial Revolution with its collaborative commons may well appear to be offering a way out of the interregnum, but in considering the future as different from the past we run the danger of overlooking their commonalities and continuities.

As Bruce Sterling points out: 'every Maker scene has some set of tribal shamans widely acknowledged as maestros. The maker Maestro sacrifices money for meaning, for mattering.'[42] The collaborative commons may or may not deliver liberation from corporate management but they are unlikely to eliminate the self-management that occurs around the power to be found in human being: 'If Motorola vanished tomorrow, few would shed a tear. However, if Linus Torvalds, creator of the Linux operating system, were to perish, there would be much rending of garments and tearing of hair.'[43] The appeal of these craftsmen engaged in 'obsessive pursuits of quality for its own sake' has proven

resilient even in the face of massive shifts in social values
– it is persistently with us. These timeless qualities hold
the same relevance for the future as they have always
done: the condition 'of being engaged', 'doing better
than just getting by'[44] and 'the individual sense of freedom and control over the world'[45] are all qualities that
we covet but struggle to hold on to in the liquid society.
When and if, through some mishap in the dystopian
future, the proverbial plug is pulled on the Internet of
Things, it is the craftsmen and their attentiveness to the
detail of life that may pull us through.

ZB 'The collaborative commons may or may not
deliver liberation from corporate management but they
are unlikely to eliminate the self-management that occurs
around the power to be found in human being', writes
Irena. That power to which Irena appeals is the impulse,
drive, desire and pursuit of excellence: that 'craftsman',
a type perhaps napping and waiting to be awakened in
each of us, described by Richard Sennett (in the study
under that very name name),[46] is guided and moved
by what Thorstein Veblen[47] almost 100 years earlier
dubbed the 'instinct of workmanship'. In his follow-
up study of cooperation, Richard Sennett (following
Amartya Sen and Martha Nussbaum) points out, however, that: 'human beings are capable of doing more than
schools, workplaces, civil organizations and political
regimes allow for . . . People's capacities for cooperation
are far greater and more complex than institutions allow
them to be'[48]; 'Cooperation is the natural habitat of the
craftsmanship or instinct of workmanship, that "obsessive pursuit of quality for its own sake".'[49] Disallowing
cooperation means depriving craftsmanship of the soil it

needs to thrive. Once exiled from its natural ecotype and transplanted onto the foreign and inhospitable ground of the machine-run, impersonal routine, a slow yet relentless wilting and fading of cooperative predispositions and skills tends to be quickly followed by the dissipation of craftsmen's ambitions. Corporate management does the job of choking the cooperative flame with the toxic smoke of competition and preventing the cooperative embers from bursting into flames by rendering interpersonal bonds shallow, short-term, prospect-less, frail, untrustworthy and unreliable (what has been destroyed in that process is 'the aura of permanence and practice of long-term employment', employees staying in one company through the whole of their working life, and industrial workers tending 'to stay put, rather than move to look for better work elsewhere').[50] Cooperation and the instinct of workmanship are born and grow together – and together they die (or rather fall flat or into a coma – they never really die). As Joke Brouwer and Sjoerd van Tuinen aver in the preface to the book they jointly edited – even if with a tad of excessive sanguinity – 'Under a thin layer of consumerism lies an ocean of generosity.'[51] Hardly ever do cooperation and craftsmanship happen to be at cross-purposes and in conflict – the craftsman being at his or her best in a society of craftsmen, a society of the 'collaborative commons' being a setting most hospitable to the practice, manifestation and display of craftsmanship.

True, cooperation among craftsmen gives rise to another human inclination: that of rivalry. But the kind of rivalry it promotes and sets into play puts it into the service of excellence and the gratifying sense of being needed by and useful to others, not of personal appropriation or enrichment. Seen from the perspective of the aggregate, its members' rivalry is in giving or adding to the collaborative commons, not in taking and detracting from it. And as Peter Sloterdijk, referring to Marcel Mauss's classic study of the gift, insists in one of the interviews included in Brouwer and Tuinen's book,[52] the 'giving' in question is not just a spontaneous outburst of generosity: it is also experienced by the giver as an obligation – though an obligation free from grudge and resentment, its fulfilment hardly ever experienced or thought of as an act of self-deprivation or self-sacrifice. In the case of a gift true to its nature, the common opposition between egoism and altruism is cancelled. That opposition is dissolved, we may say, in the state/condition/mentality/ambiance of companionship and solidarity. 'To give' means to *do* good, but also *feeling* good; the two satisfactions merge into one and are no longer distinguishable from each other – let alone at loggerheads. The first wouldn't happen without the second, and if the second comes to be, it is thanks to the first happening. Unalloyed, untainted joy derived from giving is what the editors of the quoted book and most of its contributors consider to be, as the book's subtitle implies, an antidote to a culture of greed. And that joy, let me add, is what craftsmanship, as well as cooperation, can rely on, and need to rely on and be propelled by.

Solidarity – whose spirit is best conveyed by the phrase *un pour tous, tous pour un* ('one for all, all for one'), a principle/motto ascribed by Alexander Dumas to a foursome of his musketeer heroes – is an attitude assuming, as well as manifesting in thoughts and deeds, that fusion of personal and shared wellbeing. That spirit was also an indispensable (even if silent) premise of the realization of John Rawls's theory of justice, aimed at reconciliation of freedom and equality – though the notorious difficulty of recasting Rawls's theory into social practice well illustrates the arduousness of the task of composing a social setting likely to switch the balance of probabilities firmly in solidarity's favour. Among the recorded attempts to build, purposefully, such a setting, Sennett dissects the experience of Saul Alinsky and Jane Addams in Chicago, concluding that 'ordinary experience, not policy formulas, is what counts', that 'the test of joint action should be its concrete effect on daily life, not an eventual effect such a policy promises'.[53] Both experiments 'emphasized loose rather than rigid exchanges, and made a virtue of informality'. All that was but a first step; the experiments in question set the stage for 'sociality', which stops short of – though it also enables – active cooperation. Sociality 'is not an active reaching out to others; it is mutual awareness instead of action together'. In its original meaning suggested by Simmel, sociality 'asks you to accept the stranger as a valued presence in your midst'.[54] We may say that 'sociality' is an attitude and a practice of curiosity and keeping the gate open to the risks of the unknown – an attitude of toning down, possibly suppressing, the impulse to withdraw from communication, separation, fencing off and locking the doors. What sociality enables is Hans-Georg Gadamer's 'fusion of horizons'; more, however, is needed to pave the way to 'joining forces' – that is, to *solidarity*, the Siamese twin of earnest and willing cooperation. Somewhere on the road leading from sociality to solidarity intertwined with cooperation, acquisition of new skills must happen: skills without which there will be no overcoming of fear of the 'strange' and – for that reason, therefore – baffling: the obscure, inscrutable and impermeable, therefore pregnant with disabling, paralysing uncertainty. In my terms, skills of that sort are needed to rise above instinctual *mixophobia* and into laboriously groomed *mixophilia*. The trouble is, though, that modern society tends to bar acquisition of such skills. It does it in subtle or crude ways, openly (through 'appealing-to-reason' recommendations given explicitly) or surreptitiously (through manipulating the settings of interaction and the tools of action). I'll name but two of them.

The first is the changing nature of labour relations, already mentioned above: the nowadays-prevailing social setting of a workplace, marked by its explicit frailty and impermanence and transitoriness boarding on ephemerality, prompts and encourages mutual suspicion, competitiveness and one-upmanship; keeping one's distance, avoiding fixing of bonds, taking oaths of loyalty, or long-term, let alone interminate, obligations tend to turn into commonsensical *savoir-vivre*. As a result, today's coalitions tend to be on the whole ad hoc and invariably supplied with a 'till-further-notice' clause. Instability of the employment of oneself and the others around you reduces the likelihood of digging beneath the perfunctory and one-issue, formal encounters – most contacts being (to use Martin Buber's terminology) of a *Vergegnung* (superficial mis-meetings) rather than a *Begegnung* (in-depth meetings, triggering and initiating the acquisition of mutual knowledge and understanding) character. That setting either strips the actors of the interacting skills they've already acquired and mastered, or cuts down substantially opportunities for their appropriation and development.

The second is the 'online' sector of our lives: a sector whose impact on the more and more popular world-view and *savoir-faire* is expanding and deepening day in, day out. The online half of the dual universe we inhabit offers the possibility of sweeping the challenges of cohabitation with diversity under the carpet – the kind of possibility almost inconceivable in the offline world: in a school, workplace, neighbourhood, city street. Instead of facing up to such challenges point blank and embarking on the long, bumpy and tortuous road leading from sociality to cooperation and solidarity, it tempts its visitors with the elsewhere unattainable luxury of fencing them off, ignoring and rendering irrelevant all else. Facebook 'networks of friends' are digital equivalents of massively material gated communities – though, unlike their offline replicas, they don't need CCTV and armed guards at the entrance: the fingers of the network's creator/manager/consumer, once armed with a mouse and the magic 'delete' key, wll suffice. The endemic sociality of humans is thereby cleansed of the risk of sidestepping onto the treacherous practice of collaboration and the 'fusion of horizons' with which such practice is pregnant – and morphing, eventually, into solidarity. Without accepting that risk, alas, social skills fall into disuse and oblivion – and as they do, the presence of the stranger grows yet more awesome, off-putting, repellent and frightening, while the hardships involved in an attempt to elaborate a satisfactory *modus vivendi* with that presence seem all the more overwhelming and insurmountable.

Odds against the species-wide journey towards collaborative commons look formidable indeed. Surmounting them does not, moreover, seem likely to happen spontaneously – on its own, unassisted. Watching it happening, extolling its promises and applauding its progress to date are not enough. For this to happen consistently, and to reach its completion, this process would need – yes, you've guessed it – management! Though it's probably not the kind of management we've come to know from observation and autopsy. What it needs is a novel kind of management (or self-management), made to the measure of the challenges to be faced on the road leading from competitive markets to collaborative commons, from sociality to cooperation and solidarity . . . a road thus far un-trodden, un-tested and un-mapped. Designing this kind of management is likely to require colossal thought, a stupendous volume of experimentation and prodigious amounts of monitoring. What we are slowly coming to envisage and to understand is the nature of the task. Where we are, however, still much in the dark is regarding the design and building of tools adequate to that task.

I expect Jerzy and Monika, experts and champions of managerial reform, to illuminate me on the nature of the tools fit to serve that process/effort. And Irena, the expert and champion of sustainable urbanism, to illuminate me on what can and ought to be done to create and sustain sites hospitable to such a process/effort that will increase the probability of its success.

6

Crises and consequences

Jerzy Kociatkiewicz Over the last five chapters, we have sketched an array of our hopes and fears born out of observing the present and looming crises of the organizational settings around us, which I would label (if I may be permitted this analytical indulgence) the crisis of values, the crisis of resources, and the crisis of management. The first of these would pertain to the prevalent and possibly increasing adiaphorization that Zygmunt has been mapping at least since *Modernity and the Holocaust*. The second, to our dawning realization, relates to the finitude of our planet's resources (and the fading of hopes for an imminent arrival of an abundant Space Age) and the growing visibility of the injustice inherent in the current systems for distribution of these resources. Even as we have been holding this conversation, Thomas Piketty's book[1] charting the recent growth of inequality shot to the top of bestseller lists worldwide, underscoring just how public the issue has become. And the third crisis, that of management, manifests itself in the erosion of trust in corporate structures and managerial techniques as tools for providing any semblance of fairness or ethical governance within organizations or in the marketplace. The three crises are, of course, closely related and I am aware of a certain artifice in their separation. Additionally, none of the issues are entirely new, even though their presence has been felt and appears more acutely in recent years. Yet let us assume that these crises are, indeed, as severe as they seem, and that they presage an important reconfiguration of our social and organizational arrangements. I do not think this assumption is as bold as it might seem at first glance: liquid modernity is an age of rapid and drastic changes and it is predictions of stability rather than upheaval that should strike us as adventurous and improbable. What, then, can we divine about the possible outcomes of such an imminent disruption (or, indeed, should we expect a recognizable discontinuity or just a series of gradual, though rapid, social changes)?

Zygmunt Bauman We all – or most of us – are, dear Monika and Jerzy, ever more lonely loners who ever more keep in touch (or, to express it in a better-fitting current idiom: keep connecting and disconnecting). Such a condition can only be baffling and confusing. Loneliness comes disguised as togetherness; lonesomeness, desolation, forlornness camouflaged as the advent of unbound fellowship. Togetherness amenable to entry or exit on demand or on the spur of the moment. Belonging with no strings attached, so putting paid to awkward and cumbersome initiation/admission/farewell ceremonies. The joys of belonging cleansed of the sorrows of commitment and obligation. The horrors of abandonment veneered in easiness and instantaneousness of communicability.

Pressed as we are to compensate for our communal impotence with the busyness of 'life politics', and armed with an iPhone or other smartphone in hand, pocket or bag (fewer and fewer of us would dare to leave home without it), the abomination of being left to stew in one's own juices seems to have been mitigated – indeed, made painless – by the mellifluous awareness that, at any time of day or night, there is someone, somewhere, to whom a message or a tweet can be sent and from whom we can get a response. You feel, indeed – as promised a few decades ago by the marketing catchphrase of the 'Walkman', the smartphone's precocious and primitive precursor – 'never again alone'. The unbounded freedom of cyberspace seems to make redundant surrender to a hazardous dependence on physical proximity. No wonder it is ever more difficult to find, in a waiting room, a café or any other public space, a man or a woman of any age whose eyes meet the eyes of their companions, co-sitters or passers-by instead of being fixed on the mini-screen of a hand-held gadget. Only a couple of years ago, those gadgets used to be mostly listened or talked to; nowadays, though, most of their users deploy fingers rather than ears and lips. The welcome safety of sending/receiving messages without the conversationalists looking into each other's eyes denigrates face-to-face conversation, notorious – as it is increasingly viewed – for its irksome and, through lack of practice, ever more repellent risks and hazards. It makes the practising of such conversation increasingly exacting, onerous and therefore off-putting.

Crises and consequences

JK Arlie Russell Hochschild has been studying the intersections between the personal realm and the world of work for over thirty years. In *The Managed Heart*, published in 1983, she introduced the notion of emotional labour, or the duty to feel and perform emotions (such as happiness, compassion or goodwill) that forms a significant part of work effort in any people-oriented setting. This is not the same as simply acting out emotions in interactions: most of us are unable or unwilling to behave disingenuously day after day after day, and we also prefer to interact with people we see as authentic in their conduct. In emotional labour, feelings demanded by work are internalized, genuinely felt and expressed. But such commercialization of human feelings, as Hochschild calls it in the book's subtitle, leads to alienation, estrangement from one's own feelings originating elsewhere than in the job specification. Moreover, emotional labour does not cover the full spectrum of human experience, as darker or unhappier feelings are excluded from the template of the desirable employee: no organization looks for surly, melancholic or irritable employees, even if all human beings exhibit these traits at one point or another.[2]

The continuing growth of the service sector, as well as the tendency to see more and more interactions in terms of consumer service (for example, hospital patients and university students are now commonly referred to as customers), means that emotional labour is now an issue common to most, if not all, workplaces. But, in a recent book entitled *The Outsourced Self*,[3] Hochschild argues that the cost of applying market logic to the personal and intimate spheres of life is much more prevalent, and often more damaging to the fabric of society, than just the psychological burden of emotional labour. Hochschild presents the professionalization of activities traditionally performed personally or within the community group, ranging from maintenance of familial relations to personal goal setting ('wantology') to choosing the name for one's child or even child-bearing (commercial surrogacy). Such transactions go beyond the traditionally described bounds of consumerism or commodity fetishism, and they also transcend the notion of emotional labour (though they usually involve copious amounts of it on the part of service providers), devaluing the importance of activities not funnelled through the marketplace:

> The bad news . . . is the capacity of the service market, with all its expertise, to sap self-confidence in our own capacities, and those of friends and family. The professional nameologist finds a more auspicious name than we can recall from our family tree. The professional potty trainer does the job better than the bumbling parent or helpful neighbor. . . . Happiest Day promises a more personally uplifting wedding. Happy Travels promises a more carefree holiday.[4]

The list goes on and on, but even this excerpt summarizes what seems to be the current state of self-management, understood as the management of selfhood by outside professionals. And yet it is in self-management that I would see the possible answer to the crisis of management, and possibly to the other crises as well. As Monika points out in her research on self-organizing, and as Irena notes in her description of making, other conceptualizations of self-management are not only possible, but also already practised by contemporary pioneers.

Self-management, understood as the mixture of responsibility and authority necessary to accomplish individual or collective tasks without outside supervision, is by no means a novel idea. When, in the fourteenth century, the radical preacher John Ball rhetorically asked in his fiery sermons, 'When Adam delved and Eve span who was then the gentleman?', his indignation could be interpreted (in somewhat anachronistic language) as a protest against hierarchical management as much as against the class structure. Yet, although we can find throughout history more or less contentious theories and proclamations of self-management and instituted precedents ranging from worker collectives and kibbutzim to pirate ships, I believe some of the more recent formulations of the idea could prove the most relevant for our current situation: in particular, the concept of self-managed and self-directed teams – appearing in management literature since at least the 1970s – and the currently emerging forms of self-managed online collaboration.

The need for strict hierarchy and clear organizational roles was taken for granted by most early management scholars, notably – as mentioned previously by Zygmunt – by Frederick Taylor, whose quest for the principles of scientific management involved focusing all the decision-making at the higher rungs of organizational hierarchy. The early managerial cadres hailed mostly from engineering backgrounds and were particularly comfortable with mechanistic models of organizing that eliminated ambiguity and decision-making from the lower reaches of organizational structure. Subsequent generations of managers and management scholars started asking themselves about the optimal ways of achieving control, giving birth to studies of leadership understood as a key skill to be used by successful managers. A series of experiments conducted in 1939 by a team led by Kurt Lewin acknowledged the possibility of *laissez-faire* or hands-off leadership, but concluded that, barring the abnormal situation of exceptionally skilled team members, such an approach leads to the lowest possible efficiencies and should be avoided.[5] Nevertheless, changing social and technological conditions of industrial production soon led to successful experiments with teamwork-based management – if not actually hands-off management, this at least involved semi-autonomous teams operating within larger organizational structures. In 1969, Karl Weick introduced organization theory to the concept of loose coupling, or indeterminacy in managerial rules and regulations, providing a way of safeguarding performance and allowing for flexibility demanded by changing environments.[6] Meanwhile, new ideas such as work-cell (as opposed to assembly line) manufacturing allowed the adoption of management strategies more reminiscent of Richard Sennett's craftsman's workshop than of Frederick Taylor's linear-process manufacturing.

Whether work-cell teams can be described as self-managing might be disputable, but their arrival certainly marked the beginning of an often enthusiastic discussion of team self-direction and self-management. By the 1990s, researchers reported that the number of employees working in self-managing teams had risen to 32 per cent (from a mere 2 per cent in the early 1980s).[7] These teams, despite the language of empowerment, were largely working to goals and performance indicators set by managers elsewhere in the organization, leading to accusations that the much-touted autonomy was, in most cases, largely illusory.[8] For many observers, the fault lay with companies clinging to the ideas of leadership and responsibility formulated within the context of assembly-line manufacturing. Ulla Johansson, after studying worker participation in a Swedish housing association, concluded that a much more open understanding of responsibility, involving the workers' own understanding of their organization rather than the ability or failure to achieve pre-set goals, was necessary in order to allow for employees' meaningful participation in managing their work.[9] Leadership scholars were also looking beyond the figure of a leader and the leader's skills – Robert Kelley introduced the concept of followership as the overlooked but just as important counterpart to leadership, requiring different but equally difficult skills of its practitioners.[10] Barbara Czarniawska went further, describing leaders as largely symbolic figureheads (though very important because of that role) representing collectively determined organizational processes.[11] In recent years, leadership has increasingly been understood as a collective process, likened to rhythmic music[12] or dance:[13] persistent, collective, requiring coordination, but non-hierarchical and certainly not dominated by the figure of a single master manager. If that is the case, all organizations already are to a large extent self-managed, even if resource and status distribution fails to account for the contributions of all the workers involved. Whether such an imbalance can be maintained in the longer term is a question for which we urgently need answers.

The new century has also seen tremendous growth in collaborative endeavours coordinated (and often performed) online. A very large number of projects, whether focused on writing new software – with the operating system Linux as a flagship example – or on information gathering and presentation – with Wikipedia as the most obvious poster child – demonstrate the possibility of successfully conducting largely non-hierarchical and often self-managed endeavours of great scale and complexity. Such projects – or perhaps the organizations capable of completing such projects – do not lack power structures, either emergent or preordained from the beginning (I tend to believe that power relations are an inherent feature of organizing, regardless of management configuration). But the sources of status, authority and power are not necessarily the most obvious ones. Alf Rehn, in his virtual ethnography of a group of computer pirates[14] – i.e., people committed to free distribution of software in defiance of copyright regulations – found them to be highly reminiscent of Marcel Mauss's[15] concept of a gift economy, originally identified in the indigenous civilizations of Polynesia and North America. Status and power were important and could be personally acquired, but only as rewards for continued work directed towards the common goals of the community. Very little directive power could be observed, though members with high status could influence group decisions and group behaviour. Dariusz Jemielniak described similar processes in the community of writers and editors of the Wikipedia project,[16] though there much of the work is done by anonymous or semi-anonymous users who, by definition, cannot reap any status rewards from their contributions. Nevertheless, status and prestige remain important for the most committed members of the group.

The whole collaborative phenomenon of crowd-sourcing (that is, gathering ideas and contributions towards a common project from a large and mostly anonymous community) remains relatively poorly understood, but offers both a hopeful signpost for self-management strategies of the future and a warning of the dangers we can expect to become more common. Crowd-sourcing strategies are responsible for incredible achievements in producing software and distributing knowledge. They also allow for collaborations of groups interested in goals resisted or condemned by the extant social order, currently including the above-mentioned proponents of copyright infringement, and the multi-issue activist and lifestyle grouping known as Anonymous, as well as fundamentalist terrorists.

Still, I would posit that self-management and crowd-sourcing offer a possible solution (weighed down, as all solutions are, by its own range of already visible or as yet undiscovered problems) to the crisis of management. But I also believe they can help solve the other two crises. In regard to values, new platforms of discussion and new ways of stimulating activist engagement offer an alternative to the debilitating perception that financial success has supplanted all other workable value systems. And the crisis of resources, unprecedented in that it requires concerted action on behalf of the entire global society, can only be meaningfully tackled through processes that encourage as well as allow meaningful mass participation.

Of course, Internet-based collaborations can serve only as templates: we should not forget that, even though the numbers are increasing rather rapidly, still only 40 per cent of the global population has access to the global information infrastructure.[17] And my musings offer no scenario for dismantling the currently dominant, and demonstrably harmful, structures of power and capital: the recent global wave of revolutions and uprisings shows the desperate need for meaningful change felt by many communities, but offers few examples of such meaningful change having been achieved. So, what do you think about the possible toolkits, managerial or otherwise, for the world after interregnum?

ZB In the most recent of her series of studies focused on the commercialization of human emotions,[18] Arlie Russell Hochschild juxtaposes two modes of sharing a world: 'village' and 'marketplace'. In the first, less money is changing hands than in the second – 'but more gifts are exchanged' (p. 6). In her own coming of age, Arlie Russell passed from realities of life in the little town of her birth to those of life conducted in embassies to which her father was successively assigned: 'And while I lost the feeling of belonging to a community, freshly ironed clothes and favorite meals appeared as if by magic, the final product of someone else's work.' In the village, as Arlie's Aunt Elisabeth used to say, people 'just do': 'When a need arises', she said, 'neighbours and friends don't ask themselves "Do I want to help?" They don't think about it. It's in their bones. They *just do*.' What Aunt Elisabeth must have had in mind, we may guess, was that offering the gift of their compassion and assistance came to them, as it were, 'naturally', spontaneously, unmediated by comparing 'gains' with 'costs'. The impulse to care and share was not a manifestation of their particularly altruistic predispositions, let alone an act of self-sacrifice; in a 'village' mode of togetherness, unlike in its 'marketplace' counterpart, the distinction between selfishness and selflessness was attenuated, perhaps even all but effaced: *giving* pleasure and *acquiring* pleasure (if 'only' the pleasure of acquitting oneself well of one's duty, of a job well done, or of being needed) gel to the point of becoming indistinguishable.

But, as Hochschild reminds us, while in the times of Aunt Elisabeth's voicing of her opinions and of her own early childhood 38 per cent of American workers were farmers, only 2 percent remained farmers by 2000:

> for an increasing number, family became their 'village' – but even such a shrunken variety of village, reduced to the size of a family, couldn't well withstand the march of time . . . One of the major causes of its vulnerability was 'the rise of the working woman . . . which greatly undermined the family's ability to care for itself': 'Today, 70 percent of all American children live in households where all the adults work', while first marriages have a between 40 and 50 percent chance of ending in divorce, the subsequent marriages' chances of divorce being yet higher. 'The percentage of babies born of single mothers reached 40 percent by 2011' and about 'half of American children spent at least part of their lives in single-parent households'.[19]

However seminal, these departures are but a part of the story; another, no less – if not more – important cause of the village's slow yet relentless demise is the changing character of the labour market. Quoting Robert Kuttner,[20] Hochschild notes: 'from the 1970s on, many people lost confidence that they could hold on to their jobs'. Layoffs became 'a way of life': 'Stable careers, along with pensions and benefits, were increasingly limited to the privileged.'

Traditional or learned, appropriated and deployed ways of 'getting by' all failed, one after another – together with the expectations that guided them. Neighbourhoods, treated increasingly as successive road-inns marking life's twisting itinerary, stopped well short of offering the comfort of a homely feeling of cosiness: no more than temporary stations, populated by strangers coming and going, they inspired in their fleeting visitors more suspicion and vigilance than a sense of security, let alone the courage or sheer willingness to drop anchor. One of the objects of Hochschild's in-depth study, appearing in the book under the name of Michael Haber, confides: 'Here each family is on its own. Couples move from place to place, as we do. No one feels part of anything larger. It's like we're a collection of bits and pieces floating in a vast sea . . . In the U.S. we live in a culture of want-want-want, buy-buy-buy, dump-dump-dump.'[21] So the outsourcing of selves signalled by the title of the quoted study, as well as he commercialization of emotions suggested by the title of a previous one,[22] allude to a close link between falling chances of effective self-assertion and self-management and the tendency to seek zealously market-supplied substitutes for the lost capability to cope – or just the market-offered remedies for the pains caused. This is how Hochschild herself clarifies the crucial conclusion emerging from the above quoted material, as well as an impressively long series of other, similar depth-interviews:

> The more anxious and isolated we are and the less help we receive from nonmarket sources, the more we feel tempted to fill the void with market offerings. As our California

survey shows, greater isolation results in greater demand for market services and professionals – life coaches, party planners, photograph-album assemblers – to fill in for what is missing . . .

The market is now present in our bedrooms, at our breakfast table, in our love lives, entangled in our deepest joys and sorrows . . . Ironically, the greater our dependence on the market, the greater its power to subtly undermine our intimate life . . . The bad news in this case is the capacity of the service market, with all its expertise, to sap self-confidence in our own capacities, and those of friends and family . . . Most important of all, it may prevent us from noticing how we devalue what we don't or can't buy.[23]

'Outsourcing of self' means first and foremost the forfeiture of the capability to self-manage. Deeds our parents used to do, and things they used to make themselves – by using their own skills, complemented and magnified in cooperation with kith and kin, friends and neighbours – we would no longer believe to be within our own capability to do or make things. We plug our ears at suggestions whispered by our own experience, intuition and intimations, and we don't trust sufficiently our mind's judgements – all too often for the simple enough reason that we deny value to things and acts lacking a market price tag. In line with expropriation of our craft skills and cooperating impulse, the markets robbed us of self-confidence – of trust in our own ability to do things properly, and in our own authority to pass competent judgement on the results (unless, of course, they call for nothing more than following the drawings attached to an IKEA flat-pack kit). We have been drilled and groomed to follow the market-supplied-and-purchased instructions of a 'read carefully and follow exactly' style; to seek them, watch, listen and obey. In the process, we hardly notice our ostensibly autonomous self being recycled into one more of these IKEA-kind kits – meant and destined to be assembled, dismantled and reassembled according to the unqualified and indisputable, 'open and shut' commands.

The big question – the biggest of them all, as far as the recovery, re-learning and re-appropriation of the know-how of personal and/or collective self-management skills is concerned – is whether the trend described by Hochschild can be reversed; and, if so, then how, by whom and in what way? Answers to those questions – first practical, and then theoretical – will be sought and perhaps found along the battle-line drawn between consumerist markets, eager to sell dependency, addictions and compulsion in 'freedom of choice' wrappings, and the 'collaborative commons', the natural habitat of cooperation and solidarity.

Irena Bauman Two powerful defence systems mark those battle-lines that Zygmunt speaks of: 'Disavowal' and 'Uncare', both acting as shields to consumerist markets, obscuring the sight of common horizons and resisting the pull of global solidarity that could have signalled a possible end to interregnum.

The disavowal I speak of is that of the climate change crisis and its consequences; and uncare – a term coined by Sally Weintrobe – the reason for the disavowal. Jerzy's analysis of the three current crises is correct but incomplete: it focuses on issues that sociologists and others still regard as within human control. By leaving the crisis of climate change out of our conversation, we also leave out engaging with the unpalatable possibility of 'not being able to manage'.

And yet our situation is, arguably, already unmanageable. Twenty-eight internationally renowned scientists identified and quantified a set of nine planetary boundaries within which humanity can continue to develop and thrive for generations to come.[24] Three out of these nine boundaries – the nitrogen cycle, loss of bio-diversity, and climate change – have already exceeded levels of safe operation, and two more, the phosphorus cycle and ocean acidification, are close to exceeding them. We know this but cannot manage the required change to reverse the damaging direction of travel.

This is a crisis that trumps all the others. As those boundaries are exceeded further, and the scientists predict that we are already locked into the irreversible certainty that they will, our civilization is likely to experience relentless assault as unmanageable weather-related events strike over and over again, resilience erodes, governance disintegrates, communications fail and the off line world becomes but a cherished memory, and truth is lost for most of us. Only the basics of life such as food, water, shelter and fire would matter in such a scenario. Increasingly, imagined apocalyptic scenarios match scenarios from real-life experience.[25] In these scenarios, self-management will be the only management. We are in this crisis already, as much as in all those others, but we speak of it less.

The disavowal of these real conditions forms a protective shield for business as usual and extends the period of interregnum and the likelihood of a catastrophe. According to a recent Royal Society for the

Encouragement of Arts, Manufacture and Commerce report, *A New Agenda for Climate Change*,[26] 63.9 per cent of the British population are 'unmoved' by climate change issues. A further 19.3 per cent, often termed 'deniers', 'sceptics' or 'ignorers', do not accept the full implications of the crisis in terms of their 'feelings, agency and complicity'.

Sally Weintrobe defines disavowal as a form of psychological denial that involves turning a blind eye: 'What is most disavowed with climate change is the damage our way of life is causing. Disavowal trivializes the damage, locates it as far away, discredits the messenger, or finds instant virtual "solutions" that apparently "fix" the damage. Disavowal enables us to live "as if" we see the damage, but without truly visualizing and taking in the consequences.'[27]

She suggests that the culture of disavowal has been described by different names, but always contains the fundamental ingredients of a 'sense of entitlement to a bigger portion', a 'sense of self-importance' and 'entitlement not to tolerate any difficult experience', and a 'general corruption of truth and language'. Sally Weintrobe calls these traits collectively the culture of Uncare, and suggests that there is some care and uncare in each and every one of us.[28] This culture of uncare is another shield in the armour of the status quo.

So Jerzy, Monika and Zygmunt, I ask you why, in our conversations about management, did we speak so little about the possibility of not being able to manage what we have created? Some argue that we are caught in an 'ingenuity gap' in which the world's problems have become so difficult to solve that we lack the ingenuity required to solve them.[29] Sally Weintrobe suggests that the only genuine conversation we can have about climate change, stemming from a wish to fight for sustainability and for life, is one that starts with a recognition that we are all part of a culture of uncare. I doubt that we ourselves do not care – our conversations indicate that we care deeply. Neither do I think that we are short of ideas, or closed to the ideas of others, about what the future management of society could look like. But I do think that we ourselves are caught up in a disavowal of human society losing the ability to manage itself in relation to the planet and of the planet taking over that management role. It is this disavowal that kept our discourse short of being disruptive – an unfired cannon that could have made a dent in the barricades but failed to fulfil its intended function.

It is difficult to imagine how hospitable space for a move from competitive markets to collaborative commons, sociality to cooperation towards solidarity, could be created in a society that is in disavowal of the consequences of its own actions, and operating in a culture of uncare. Hope lies with the handful – admittedly, one that is growing – of the caring and the resilient 'architects of the collaborative commons' (whom we acknowledged throughout our conversations), who are proactively developing practical solutions of mitigation and adaptation and innovative resilient systems that will allow us to regain control over our collective destiny. They are opening the doors into a world so attractive that they might just be able to turn disavowal into desire, and uncare into embrace.

Until conversation takes place between the part of us that cares and the part of us caught up with uncare, their task will continue to be an uphill struggle – 'when dominated by uncare ourselves, we are not able to listen to others or ourselves in a way that will touch us'.[30]

Such a conversation with oneself seems an achievable management task and may be the gesture that can, and ought to, be made to create and sustain the sites hospitable to the collaborative commons, and to increase the probability of its success – one answer to the many questions posed by these conversations.

JK The crisis of caring is, indeed, a global malady that threatens to devour not just our society, but the ecological system of our planet. But, regardless of its catastrophic potential, it is important to remember its roots in, and its dependence on, the processes of adiaphorization prevalent throughout the liquid modern societies. The very mechanisms Zygmunt has described in *Modernity and the Holocaust*, deployed across a wide range of organizations in the name of efficiency and professionalization, foster uncare not only in the workplace, but also in relation to the wider environment. It comes as no surprise that numerous studies suggest links between sociopathy and personal success in contemporary management hierarchies:[31] being good at adiaphorization is a key performance indicator for liquid modern organizations.

And yet, as Lévinas and Zygmunt both insist, the impulse of boundless responsibility for the Other needs to be suppressed precisely because it is so overwhelming, and yet so important for our humanity. Even as we continue to exercise uncare, we all carry the potential for caring. What we need are social, and managerial, tools to realize this potential. This is the challenge and the promise of collaborative commons: the possibility of working together for the common good that we crave but, so far, find very difficult to realize.

Monika Kostera   Loners in a stranger world ... You write, Zygmunt: 'Once exiled from its natural ecotype and transplanted onto foreign and inhospitable ground of the machine-run, impersonal routine, a slow yet relentless wilting and fading of cooperative predispositions and skills tends to be fast followed by the dissipation of craftsmen ambitions.' In answer to Jerzy's call for possible managerial toolkits for the interregnum, able to deal with the three terminal systemic crises, and also having in mind my favourite blend of Utopia, reflecting the desire for a return to our natural ecotype, I would like to propose a new kind of gardener society. In your description, Zygmunt, of the gardener society of the past,[32] the garden is seen as the ultimate harmony, where perfect order rules, and the gardener has a vision of the totality, after which he or she carefully and forcefully moulds the actual life of the plants and manages their strivings. Such a garden does not sustain itself; it is constantly the object of control, supervision and design. The gardener cares for the garden by imposing and maintaining order.

The new gardener that I propose as the model of (self-)management for the interregnum is a much more modest craftsman, who, in Irena's words, is concerned not about control and ownership, but sharing, collaboration and 'obsessive pursuits of quality for its own sake'.

Zygmunt proposes solidarity, sociality and mixophilia as important organizing principles of the society after the interregnum. A management able to rely on these principles needs to recognize the rules not of competition but of collaboration, as you say, Zygmunt: 'a novel kind of management (or self-management), made to the measure of the challenges to be faced on the road leading from competitive markets to collaborative commons, from sociality to cooperation and solidarity'. The kind of management that emerges from these reflections and ideas as a possibility is, I think, very much in line with the tradition of self-management, outlined by Jerzy, from the garden of Eden (*sic*!) to kibbutzim (not so far away from the gardens, either), and including the central feature of such management – *responsibility*. A self-management based on the idea of the craftsman-gardener aims not at control – by means of the standardization, synchronization and specialization typical of modern management[33] – but at an active taking of responsibility,[34] resulting in a concern for *quality*, not quantity. Quality is a central feature of craftsmanship, as Irena points out.

Mihaela Kelemen discusses different ideas and practices connected with quality, pointing out the slogan- and marketing-oriented uses of the term in contrast to the actual practices, and shows how the experience of quality is rooted in ethics and the culture of work.[35] Quality uprooted from its context fails to become an authentically good project. It needs a democratic approach in order to become one. In a similar vein, Adrian Wilkinson and Hugh Willmott promote an understanding of quality that would encompass work processes, as well as organizational decision-making, structures, internal division of labour, and a questioning of fundamental assumptions.[36] Such a radical holistic approach to quality brings forward features of organizations that have been more or less forcefully eradicated during modernity:[37] variety and alterity.[38] If we want a deep and experienced quality, a society of thriving variety and mixophilia, we need a kind of management that is sensitive towards it and simply able to embrace it – in line with the famous Ashby Law of Requisite Variety,[39] which states that a controlling subsystem needs to embrace a certain minimal variety in order to control a system of a given number of states, or, in terms of management, that in order to manage a diverse organization, management needs increasingly to embrace variety, too.[40] Therefore, in the new ecological Arcadia, the craftsman gardener will not be one for weeding out all difference, dominating the landscape or obsessive ordering but, rather, for taking care of the weaker plants, making room for all species, watering, making sure that the plants share the resources to achieve a lively and diverse effect.

Coda

Jerzy Kociatkiewicz   Our aim throughout this conversation has been to mull over issues facing the people in 21st-century organizations, rather than to provide a clear diagnosis or ready-made tools for action. It is thus hardly surprising that what we arrived at is not a coherent snapshot or complete agreement, but rather a range of viewpoints and ideas. After all, today's world is hardly coherent, even as the issues that face us, as Irena reminds us, increasingly demand concerted, global action if we are to have any hope of overcoming the already extant crises as well as the expected maladies to come.

Despite all our talk of ideals and utopias, our assessment of the current situation appears to veer towards the grim – at best, an interregnum following the failure of the modern model of constant progress; at worst a runaway train hurtling towards a planet-wide catastrophe. We agree that a change is needed, and that the sooner we realize the utter unsustainability of the currently prevalent model of social and economic relations, the better chance we have of salvaging the planet and the achievements of our civilization not just for ourselves, but for generations to come. Zygmunt sees hope in learning to collaborate for the common good and in the recent resurgence in popularity of 'the commons', be they physical or virtual. Irena argues for open conversation and for recognition of the profound duty of caring – caring not just for the sentient Other, but for the entirety of our experienced world, or environment. Monika proposes coupling care with responsibility, and with the holistic commitment to quality of our actions as well as outcomes, organizations as well as their products.

All of these are important insights we need to take to heart. But Irena also raises a crucial question that needs to be answered before we accept any ways in which management could contribute to building a fairer, better, more sustainable society: will we be able to manage at all? Might it not be the case that our recklessness, cold-heartedness and greed have already destroyed any possibility of controlling the outcome of our actions?

The word 'management', the *Oxford English Dictionary* tells us, comes from the Italian *maneggiare*, a term that in medieval times referred mostly to mastering (handling, directing, exercising) a horse. It serves as a useful image for the relationship presupposed by much of contemporary management literature: the successful manager is one who is able to enforce his (more rarely, her) vision, making employees follow the prescribed course of action. Indeed, there is an entire industry of popular and lucrative courses teaching would-be leaders to control horses in preparation for using the same skills to direct underlings in corporate settings.[1]

And yet, as Heather Höpfl, the great management scholar who tragically passed away last year, kept reminding us, the rhetoric of control is only one way of understanding management. To manage can mean not only to handle, but also to cope, and organizations are as much sites of compassion and poetic ambivalence as they are of hierarchical order and symbolic violence.[2] While control-focused management might not be an effective way of dealing with the challenges that face us and our planet, it does not mean that we are powerless in the face of the frightening consequences of our past and current actions.

There is little reason to believe the crisis of management will not be overcome. In spite of the dangers and tribulations before us, I remain upbeat about the possibility of not only building, but also managing the caring relations that we all agree are increasingly necessary. Rather than worry about the very possibility of managing, we need to find new ways for self-management and for managing *with* other inhabitants of the planet and the planet itself. The results of such a search cannot, of course, be predicted, which is the reason none of us ventured to offer any firm recipes for managing in the world after interregnum. But if we are to hope that such solutions can be found, we need not only dire warnings of impeding catastrophe, but also dreams and utopias to make that quest worthwhile.

Monika Kostera

In 1969, Joni Mitchell sang that we are all 'stardust' and 'golden', dating back a billion years, yearning to return to the Garden of Eden.[3] The song, a hymn about the Woodstock festival, captures not only the spirit of the festival and youth culture of that time, but something much more persistent, constant in the dreams of humanity – the longing for our common green mother, the utopia of Arcadia, which I addressed earlier in our conversation. I grew up in a poor semi-rural suburb of Warsaw, populated by workers and a social group known in Poland as worker–farmers. All the inhabitants of our street had gardens, whether large or small, and some had whole – even if not very large – farms, complete with horses and carts. I used to believe that under the sidewalks lining our street there grew a lush, unruly garden, humming and ready to spring up and devour all the attempts at ordering and taming imposed upon it by people. Unlike the young rebels of Paris 1968, I did not see a beach there, but intense, vital weeds, palpable, visible, springing from between the pavement slabs. The sidewalk rested on an ocean of boisterous green, like a raft on a treacherous, seemingly calm water.

There is a collection of pictures, very popular recently in the social media, showing nature reclaiming space civilized, or colonized, by humans.[4] It presents a tree in California growing through an old piano; abandoned train tracks in Paris, all in bloom; an abandoned shopping centre in Bangkok filled with water and serving as home for a plenitude of fish; the Ukrainian radioactive city Pripyat, literally grown over by a thick, lush forest – wild gardens bursting out in hotel rooms, railway stations, temples and ships. They remind me, indeed, of your own garden, Zygmunt, where the lush and vibrant variety bustles with life and insubordination. The luxuriant roses reach out in all directions, green shoots whisk almost orgiastically throughout the whole area, not stopping for paths modestly designed for human feet, or for the robust, voluminous trees, or, indeed, for each other. Yours is, however, by no means a neglected or uncared-for garden. It reminds me very much of Claude Monet's painting from 1902, *Garden Path at Giverny*, where what you can see is clearly a garden, not a wilderness – Monet dedicated much effort and funds to improvements in his garden, which served as a model for this, and many other, paintings – but a garden where patterns or groupings look anything but imposed, and where each plant seems to have a life of its own, while working together with its neighbours to create a shifting and unpredictable – as well as far from perfect – harmony. The line of sight in the painting is clearly that of a grown-up human; the gardener oversees and visibly takes delight in his garden. The delight is tinged with responsibility: a work well done, a responsibility to carry but also to cherish, open before him both a path intended for human feet and a sight of immense vitality that shows the garden's self-determination, where he is but a respectful, if welcome, guest, and not a sovereign or designer. He is inviting, not structuring; and letting grow, not motivating; he is inspiring, not planning; caring, not controlling. In terms of ideology, this kind of self-management parts company with the ideals of the bourgeois French revolution – 'Liberté, Égalité, Fraternité' – but does so without enmity or clash; it develops them, by embracing the motto of the Yugoslav partisans 'bratstvo i jedinstvo' ('brotherhood [or, as I prefer: siblinghood] and unity'), reclaimed for and re-adapted to the new era. Liberty, a bold and grand idea for increasing the social participation and rights of all citizens, has become appropriated and re-interpreted by liquid modernity to mean lack of responsibility for the Other, lack of compassion and social justice. In the name of freedom, wars have been, and still are, fought

– devastating, disastrous to civilians, catastrophic from the point of view of world peace and political balance. Equality, in its guise as an idea of social fairness – as in Louis Blanc's famous slogan, 'De chacun selon ses moyens, à chacun selon ses besoins' ('From each according to their means, to each according to their needs'),[5] was a project embraced by community-orientated and socialist movements, including the cooperative movement. However, in solid modernity it has been made to mean, by states with total or totalitarian aspirations, *equalization,* an imposition of standards of normality, whereby people of certain races, skin colour, gender, sexual orientation, etc., were stigmatized, forcibly assimilated or even murdered. To get rid of these associations, the partisan motto – which may be reformulated as 'solidarity and sociality', as you advocate, Zygmunt – seems to be a good dictum for a self-managed future. Siblinghood – solidarity – is a loyalty to, and responsibility for, one another, or, in your words, 'aimed at reconciliation of freedom and equality'. Unity – sociality, again to borrow your words, Zygmunt, is 'an attitude and a practice of curiosity and keeping the gate open to the risks of the unknown'. They both accept – nay, *assume* – a radical variety and alterity, the ultimate difference of the Other, for whom, in Lévinasian[6] terms, we are to assume responsibility – a moment from which the ethical impulse is born, as well as a sense of absolute relatedness and also of absolute salvation. It is through the Other that we acquire meaning; it is also through and for the Other that we lose that kind of freedom which is linked to thinking only in terms of one's own interest and good. Alterity, the unknown and unknowable, unmanageable *otherness,* difference, of the Other, in that sense both threatens and liberates us as moral beings. Therefore, I believe in a self-management based on ideals of solidarity and sociality, siblinghood and unity, for the affirmation and embracing of alterity.

Notes

1 On interregnum, meso-level organizing and the city

1 Cf. Monika Kostera and Jerzy Kociatkiewicz (eds.) (2014) *Liquid Organization: Zygmunt Bauman and Organization Theory*. London: Routledge.

2 Zygmunt Bauman (1998) *Work, Consumerism, and the New Poor*. Cambridge: Polity.

3 Zygmunt Bauman (2011) *Collateral Damage*. Cambridge: Polity.

4 Guy Standing (2011) *The Precariat: The New Dangerous Class*. London: Bloomsbury Academic.

5 Mike Savage, Fiona Devine, Niall Cunningham *et al.* (2013) 'A New Model of Social Class? Findings from the BBC's Great British Class Survey Experiment', *Sociology* 47/2: 219–50.

6 Charles Handy (1989) *The Age of Unreason*. Cambridge, MA: Harvard University Press.

7 Zygmunt Bauman (2012) 'Times of Interregnum', *Ethics & Global Politics* 5/1: 49–56.

8 John Lanchester (2013) 'Are We Having Fun Yet?' *London Review of Books* 35/13: 3–8.

9 E.g. Ralf Bosen (2013) 'Foxconn Accused of Exploiting Workers in Europe', *Deutsche Welle*, retrieved from: www.dw.de/foxconn-accused-of-exploiting-workers-in-europe/a-17132689.

10 Kevin Core (2013) 'Asda Chief: Cheap Food "Not to Blame for Horsemeat"', BBC Radio 4, retrieved from: www.bbc.co.uk/news/business-21805530.

11 Clean Clothes Campaign (2013) 'Labels Primark and Mango Found after Factory Collapse Bangladesh', retrieved from www.cleanclothes.org/news/press-releases/2013/04/24/labels-primark-and-mango-found-after-factory-collapse-bangladesh.

12 Monika Kostera (2014) *Occupy Management! Inspirations and Ideas for Self-management and Self-organization*. London: Routledge.

13 Higher Education Statistics Agency (2013) 'Students by Subject of Study, First Year Indicator, Mode of Study and Level of Study 2011/12', retrieved from: www.hesa.ac.uk/dox/dataTables/studentsAndQualifiers/download/subject1112.xls.

14 Benjamin Powell and Matt Zwolinski (2011) 'The Ethical and Economic Case Against Sweatshop Labor: A Critical Assessment', *Journal of Business Ethics* 107/4: 449–72.

15 Emmanuel Lévinas (1999) *Alterity and Transcendence*. London: The Athlone Press.

16 Bauman, 'Times of Interregnum'.

17 Krzysztof Obłój (1986) *Zarządzanie: Ujęcie praktyczne*. Warsaw: PWE.

18 Kostera, *Occupy Management!*.

19 Victor Turner (1974) *Dramas, Fields, and Metaphors: Symbolic Action in Human Society*. Ithaca, NY: Cornell University Press.

20 BBC 4 (2014) *Hidden Killers*. Retrieved from: www. bbc.co.uk/programmes/b03n2yxq.

21 Lévinas, *Alterity and Transcendence*.

22 Knud Løgstrup (1997) *The Ethical Demand*. Notre Dame, IN: University of Notre Dame Press.

23 Max Weber (1947) *The Theory of Social and Economic Organization*, translated by A. M. Henderson and Talcott Parsons. London: Collier Macmillan Publishers.

24 Cary Cooper, as quoted in Stefan Stern (2013) 'Work's Not Working: Unlimited Leave Could Be the Solution', *Guardian*, retrieved from: www. theguardian.com/commentisfree/2013/jul/12/work-not-working-unlimited-leave.

25 Melissa Mayer, as quoted in Margaret Ryan (2013) 'Teleworking: The Myth of Working from Home', *BBC News*, retrieved from: www.bbc.co.uk/news/magazine-21588760.

26 Benjamin Barber (2013) *If Mayors Ruled the World: Dysfunctional Nations, Rising Cities*. New Haven: Yale University Press.

27 Ibid., p. 3.

28 Ibid., p. 4

29 Ibid., p. 9

30 Ibid., p. 4.

31 Ibid., p. 13.

32 Lewis Mumford (1937/2011) 'What is a City?', in Richard T. LeGates and Frederic Stout (eds.) *The City Reader, Fifth Edition*. Abingdon: Routledge (pp. 91–6), p. 94.

33 Barbara Czarniawska (2002) *A Tale of Three Cities: Or the Glocalization of City Management*. Oxford: Oxford University Press.

34 Zygmunt Bauman and Carlo Bordoni (2014) *State of Crisis.* Cambridge: Polity.

35 Zygmunt Bauman (2003) *City of Fears, City of Hopes.* London: Goldsmiths College, p. 31.

36 Jerzy Kociatkiewicz and Monika Kostera (2010) 'Experiencing the Shadow: Organizational Exclusion and Denial within Experience Economy', *Organization* 17/2: 257–82.

37 World Health Organization (2014) 'Urban Population Growth', retrieved from: www.who.int/gho/urban_health/situation_trends/urban_population_growth_text/en.

38 United Nations Human Settlements Programme (2012) 'State of the World's Cities 2012/2013', retrieved from: http://sustainabledevelopment.un.org/content/documents/745habitat.pdf.

39 Mark Davis (2006) *Planet of Slums: Urban Involution and the Informal Working Class.* London: Verso.

40 Edward Glaeser (2011) *Triumph of the City: How Our Greatest Invention Makes Us Richer, Smarter, Greener, Healthier, and Happier.* New York: The Penguin Press.

41 Benjamin Barber (2013) 'Poverty in Abundance: Is Corruption the Answer?' *Social Change Review* 11/1: 37–43, p. 43.

42 See, e.g., Avishai Margalit (1998) *The Decent Society.* Boston, MA: Harvard University Press.

43 Barber, *If Mayors Ruled the World.*

44 Martin Buber (1917) *Ereignisse und Begegnungen.* Leipzig: Insel Verlag.

45 Quentin Skinner (1998) *Liberty before Liberalism.* Cambridge: Cambridge University Press.

46 Hegel (1967) *Philosophy of Right*. London: Oxford University Press.
47 Skinner, *Liberty*, pp. 116–17.
48 Ibid., p. 104.
49 Ibid., p. 107.
50 Ibid., pp. 82–4.
51 Joseph S. Nye (1971) *Peace in Parts: Integration and Conflict in Regional Organizations*. Boston, MA: Little, Brown.

2 Management without managers?

1 Robert Jackall (2009) *Moral Mazes: The World of Corporate Managers*. Oxford and New York: Oxford University Press.
2 The term 'Panarchy' was first coined by the Belgian philosopher, economist and botanist Paul Emil de Puydt in 1860, referring to a specific form of governance (-archy) that would encompass (pan-) all others.
3 Lance H. Gunderson and C. S. Holling (eds.) (2002) *Panarchy: Understanding Transformations in Human and Natural Systems*. Washington, DC: Island Press.
4 Brian Walker and David Salt (2006) *Resilience Thinking: Sustaining Ecosystems and People in a Changing World*. Washington, DC: Island Press.
5 Jeremy Rifkin (2011) *The Third Industrial Revolution*. New York: Palgrave Macmillan.
6 Ibid.
7 Edward O. Wilson (1984). *Biophilia*. Cambridge, MA: Harvard University Press.
8 Edward O. Wilson (1992) *The Diversity of Life*. New York: W. W. Norton, p. 350.

9 Jeff Howe coined this phrase in his article published in 2006: 'The Rise of Crowdsourcing', *Wired*, retrieved from: http://archive.wired.com/wired/archive/14.06/crowds.html.

10 Bruno Latour and Steve Woolgar (1979) *Laboratory Life: The Social Construction of Scientific Facts.* Beverly Hills: Sage.

11 Bruno Latour (2005) *Reassembling the Social: An Introduction to Actor-Network Theory.* Oxford: Oxford University Press.

12 E.g. Bruno Latour (1996) *Aramis, or the Love of Technology.* Cambridge, MA: Harvard University Press; John Law (1994) *Organizing Modernity.* Oxford: Blackwell.

13 E.g. Michel Callon (ed.) (1998) *The Laws of the Markets.* Oxford: Blackwell; Bruno Latour (2004) *Politics of Nature: How to Bring the Sciences into Democracy.* Cambridge, MA: Harvard University Press.

14 Richard Wilkinson and Kate Pickett (2009) *The Spirit Level: Why Equality is Better for Everyone.* London: Penguin Books.

15 Zygmunt Bauman (2013) *Does the Richness of the Few Benefit Us All?* Cambridge: Polity.

16 Roland Berger, David Grusky, Tobias Raffel, Geoffrey Samuels and Christopher Wimer (eds.) (2010) *The Inequality Puzzle: European and US Leaders Discuss Rising Income Inequality.* Heidelberg: Springer.

17 I am well aware it still lingers in the names, though not in the programmes, of a number of European political parties. That is not the discursive presence I envisage in the above comment.

18 Manuel Castells (1996) *The Rise of the Network Society*. Oxford: Blackwell.

19 Pierre Bourdieu (1998) *Acts of Resistance: Against the New Myths of Our Time*. Cambridge: Polity.

20 Pierre Bourdieu (1996) 'Le Nord et le Midi: contribution à une analyse de l'effet Montesquieu'. Lecture at the University of Freiburg, October 1996.

21 Tietmeyer, as quoted in Bourdieu, *Acts of Resistance*, p. 46.

22 Bourdieu, *Acts of Resistance*, p. 50.

23 Ibid.

24 Antonio Gramsci (1971) *Selections from the Prison Notebooks*. New York: International Publishers.

25 Keith Tester (2009) 'Pleasure, Reality, the Novel and Pathology', *Journal of Anthropological Psychology* 21: 23–6.

26 Oswald Spengler (1918/1991) *Decline of the West*. Oxford: Oxford University Press.

27 Bourdieu, *Acts of Resistance*, p. 55.

28 Tomas Sedlacek (2011) *Economics of Good and Evil: The Quest for Economic Meaning from Gilgamesh to Wall Street*. Oxford: Oxford University Press.

29 Ibid., p. 161.

30 Roman Batko (2013) *Golem, Midas, Awatar, Złoty Cielec: Organizacja publicznej w płynnej nowoczesności*. Warsaw: Sedno.

31 Zygmunt Bauman (1991) *Modernity and the Holocaust*. Cambridge: Polity.

3 The organization of the global and the local

1 Zygmunt Bauman (2013) *Does the Richness of the Few Benefit Us All?* Cambridge: Polity, p. 96.

2 E. F. Schumacher (1993) *Small is Beautiful: Study of*

Economics as if People Mattered. London: Vintage, pp. 22–3.

3 Ibid., p. 22.

4 BBC (2013) 'EU Agrees to Cap Bankers' Bonuses', *BBC Business News*, retrieved from: www.bbc. co.uk/news/business-21608938.

5 Ibid.

6 BBC (2010) 'Q&A: Basel Rules on Bank Capital – Who Cares?' *BBC Business News*, retrieved from: www.bbc.co.uk/news/business-11281750.

7 'US Philanthropists Make Charitable Donations Worth $3.4bn in 2013' (2014) *Guardian*, retrieved from: www.theguardian.com/society/2014/jan/01/donations-us-philanthropists-2013.

8 Popular Resistance (2014) 'Denmark Outraged over Sale of Energy Co. to Goldman Sachs', *Daily Movement News and Resources*, retrieved from: www.popularresistance.org/denmark-outraged-over-sale-of-energy-co-to-goldman-sachs.

9 Robert Skidelsky and Edward Skidelsky (2012) *How Much is Enough? The Love of Money, and the Case for the Good Life*. London: Penguin Books.

10 Ibid., p. 4.

11 William Thomas and Florian Znaniecki (1984) *Polish Peasants in Europe and America*. Chicago: University of Illinois Press.

12 J. M. Coetzee (2008) *Diary of a Bad Year*. London: Penguin Books.

13 Ibid., p. 79.

14 Lewis Mumford (1934) *Technics and Civilization*. New York: Harcourt, Brace and Co., p. 77.

15 Ibid.

16 Lewis Mumford (1946) *Values for Survival: Essays,*

Addresses, and Letters on Politics and Education.
New York: Harcourt Brace and Co., p. 183.

17 Lewis Mumford as quoted in: Carey Winfrey (1977) 'Lewis Mumford Remembers', *New York Times*, 6 July.

18 The University of Edinburgh (2011) 'Why is Employability Important?', retrieved from: www.employability.ed.ac.uk/Why.

19 Donald N. McCloskey (1985) *The Rhetoric of Economics.* Madison: University of Wisconsin Press.

20 Jim E. H. Bright and Robert G. L. Pryor (2005) 'The Chaos Theory of Careers: A User's Guide', *The Career Development Quarterly* 53/4: 291–303, p. 296.

21 Zygmunt Bauman (2011) *Liquid Modern Challenges to Education.* Padua: Padua University Press, p. 32.

22 Tomas Sedlacek (2011) *Economics of Good and Evil: The Quest for Economic Meaning from Gilgamesh to Wall Street.* Oxford: Oxford University Press.

23 Kenwyn K. Smith (1982) 'Philosophical Problems in Thinking about Organizational Change', in Paul S. Goodman (ed.) *Change in Organizations.* San Fransisco: Jossey-Bass, pp. 316–74.

24 Amir Levy (1986) 'Second-order Planned Change: Definition and Conceptualization', *Organizational Dynamics* 15/1: 5–23.

25 Pasquale Gagliardi (1986) 'The Creation and Change of Organizational Cultures: A Conceptual Framework', *Organization Studies* 7/2: 117–34.

26 Royston Greenwood and C. R. Hinings (1988) 'Organizational Design Types, Tracks and the Dynamics of Strategic Change', *Organization Studies* 9/3: 293–316.

27 Barbara Czarniawska-Joerges (1993) *The Three-Dimensional Organization: A Constructionist View.* Lund: Studentlitteratur, p. 20, original emphasis.

28 Karl E. Weick (1995) *Sensemaking in Organizations.* Thousand Oaks: Sage.

29 Czarniawska-Joerges, *The Three-Dimensional Organization*, p. 30.

30 Linda Smircich and Gareth Morgan (1982) 'Leadership: The Management of Meaning', *Journal of Applied Behavioral Studies* 1/8: 257–73.

4 Utopian hopes

1 Fredric Jameson (2005) *Archeologies of the Future: The Desire Called Utopia and Other Science Fictions.* London: Verso.

2 Zygmunt Bauman (1973) *Socialism: The Active Utopia.* London: George Allen & Unwin, p. 12.

3 Zygmunt Bauman (2003) 'Utopia with no Topos', *History of the Human Sciences* 16/1: 11–25; pp. 23–4.

4 Thomas Kuhn (1962) *The Structure of Scientific Revolutions.* Chicago: University of Chicago Press.

5 Michel Foucault (1969) *The Archaeology of Knowledge.* London: Routledge.

6 John Kenneth Galbraith (1958) *The Affluent Society.* Boston, MA: Houghton Mifflin.

7 Joseph de Maistre, letter of 15 Aug. 1811 ('Toute nation a le gouvernement qu'elle mérite') in *Lettres et opuscules inedits* (1811/1851), Vol. I, no. 53, reprinted in Fred R. Shapiro (ed.) *The Yale Book of Quotations* (New Haven: Yale University Press, 2006), p. 485.

8 Tim Jackson (2013) 'The Trouble with Productivity',

in Anna Coote and Jane Franklin (eds.) *Time on Our Side: Why We All Need a Shorter Working Week*. London: New Economics Foundation (pp. 25–31), p. 25.

9 Jared Diamond (2011) *Collapse: How Societies Choose to Fail and Succeed*. New York: Penguin.

10 Jim Dator (2009) 'The Unholy Trinity, Plus One', *Journal of Futures Studies* 13/3: 33–48.

11 James Lovelock (2006) *The Revenge of Gaia*. London: Penguin.

12 Chris Rapley (2013) 'Foreword', in Sally Weintrobe (ed.) *Engaging with Climate Change: Psychoanalytic and Interdisciplinary Perspectives*. Oxford: Routledge (pp. xix–xxi).

13 Ibid., p. xx.

14 *Time of the Wolf (Le Temps du Loup)*, directed by Michael Haneke, released in 2003. Set in France at an undisclosed time, the film follows the story of a family, Georges, Anne and their two children, following an unspecified catastrophe; it explores relationships between people when social order breaks down.

15 *The Road*, directed by John Hillcoat, released in 2009.

16 Cormac McCarthy (2006) *The Road*. New York: Alfred A. Knopf.

17 Clayton M. Christensen (1997) *The Innovator's Dilemma*. Boston, MA: Harvard Business School Press.

18 *Blade Runner*, directed by Ridley Scott, released in 1982; loosely based on the 1968 novel *Do Androids Dream of Electric Sheep?* by Philip K. Dick. *Blade Runner* continues to reflect modern trends and

concerns such as genetic modification, artificial intelligence, desire for life and love. It was voted the best science fiction film ever made in a poll of sixty eminent world scientists conducted in 2004.

19 Michel Houellebecq (2005) *The Possibility of an Island*. London: Phoenix. The book explores a post-apocalyptic world in which science and technology enable human immortality through cloning and isolation but the longing for love remains the key motivation for action.

20 John Grey and Jared Diamond (2013) 'Traditional Societies and Myths of the Future', *New Statesman* online, 31 January 2013, retrieved from: www.newstatesman.com/culture/culture/2013/01/jared-diamond-traditional-societies-and-myths-future.

21 Mark Lynas (2008) *Six Degrees: Our Future on a Hotter Planet*. Washington, DC: National Geographic Society, pp. 235–6.

22 Carl Cederström and André Spicer (2015) *The Wellness Syndrome*. Cambridge: Polity.

23 Monika Kostera (2014) *Occupy Management! Inspirations and Ideas for Self-management and Self-organization*. London: Routledge.

24 Battista Alberti, as quoted in: Ernest Becker (1973) *The Denial of Death*. New York: Free Press, p. 113.

25 George Orwell (1949) *1984*. London: Secker and Warburg.

26 Aldous Huxley (1932/2006) *Brave New World*. New York: HarperCollins.

5 Craftsmanship

1 Michel Foucault (1967/1997) 'Of Other Spaces: Utopias and Heterotopias' in Neil Leach (ed.)

Rethinking Architecture: A Reader in Cultural Theory. London: Routledge (pp. 330–6), p. 332.

2 Samuel R. Delany (1976/1996) *Trouble on Triton: An Ambiguous Heterotopia*. Hanover: Wesleyan University Press. The subtitle echoed Ursula LeGuin's novel *Dispossessed: An Ambiguous Utopia*.

3 Richard Florida (2002) *The Rise of the Creative Class*. New York: Basic Books.

4 Alex Proud (2014) 'Why this "Shoreditchification" of London Must Stop', retrieved from: www.telegraph. co.uk/men/thinking-man/10561607/Why-this-Shoreditchification-of-London-must-stop.html. Alex Eror (2014) 'In Defence of the Shoreditchification of London', retrieved from: www.telegraph.co.uk/ men/thinking-man/10571976/In-defence-of-the-Shoreditchification-of-London.html.

5 Richard Sennett (2008) *The Craftsman*. New Haven: Yale University Press.

6 Zygmunt Bauman and Stanisław Obirek (2013) *O Bogu i Człowieku Rozmowy*. Krakow: Wydawnictwo Literackie, p. 45; Zygmunt Bauman and Stanislaw Obirek (2015) *Of God and Man*. Cambridge: Polity.

7 C. Wright Mills (1959) *The Sociological Imagination*. New York: Oxford University Press.

8 Andrzej Bursa memorably and satirically conflated the perspectives of the poet and the bureaucrat: 'A poet suffers for the multitudes / from 10 to 1:20 / At 11:10 his bladder gets full' (translation JK): Andrzej Bursa (1993) *Luiza i inne utwory* (*Luiza and other works*). Warsaw: Anagram.

9 Edward A. Kundla (1998) *Creativity and Craftsmanship in Modeling*, AIA Small Project

Forum Report 14, retrieved from: www.aia.org/aiau cmp/groups/aia/documents/pdf/aiab091888.pdf.

10 Michel Foucault (2000) 'Different Spaces', in James Faubion (ed.) *Aesthetics, Method, and Epistemology: Essential Works of Foucault 1954–1984.* Vol. II. New York: Penguin, p. 178.

11 Daniel Hjorth (2005) 'Organizational Entrepreneurship: With de Certeau on Creating Heterotopias (or Spaces for Play)', *Journal of Management Inquiry* 14/4: 386–98.

12 Kent Hansen, as quoted in Kent Hansen and Christine Buhl Andersen (2001), p. 57, as quoted in Hjorth, 'Organizational Entrepreneurship', p. 394.

13 Hjorth, 'Organizational Entrepreneurship', p. 394.

14 Research project on alternative organizations supported by the European Union Marie Curie Fellowship Programme: FP7, 627429 ECOPREN FP7/PEOPLE 2013 IEF.

15 Harry Braverman (1974) *Labor and Monopoly Capital: The degradation of Work in the Twentieth Century.* New York: Monthly Review Press.

16 Roy Jacques (1996) *Manufacturing the Employee: Management Knowledge from the 19th to 21st Centuries.* London: Sage Publications.

17 Jeremy Rifkin (2014) *The Zero Marginal Cost Society: The Internet of Things, The Collaborative Commons, and the Eclipse of Capitalism.* New York: Palgrave Macmillan.

18 Antonio Gramsci (1971) *Selections from the Prison Notebooks.* New York: International Publishers.

19 Rifkin, *The Zero Marginal Cost Society*, p. 16.

20 Ibid., p. 18.

21 Ibid., p. 43.
22 Ibid., p. 23.
23 Ibid., p. 74.
24 Ibid., p. 19.
25 Ibid.
26 Andrew Mawson (2008) *The Social Entrepreneur: Making Communities Work*. London: Atlantic Books.
27 Ibid.
28 Andrew Mawson, Santiago Bell and many others went on to build the Bromley-by-Bow Centre in East London that today employs over 100 staff and runs over 100 activities each week in high-quality purpose-designed buildings. It has transformed the derelict 3-acre recreation ground which surrounds the buildings into a beautiful, award-winning community park. It has helped to establish a £300 million local housing company which now manages over 8,000 properties across the Poplar estate. It has become a catalyst demonstrating practical social innovation and changes, and has made an impact not just locally but nationally and internationally.
29 Retrieved from www.bill-strickland.org.
30 Patrick Suskind (1985) *Perfume, The Story of a Murderer*. London: Hamish Hamilton.
31 From *Andrei Rublev*, a film directed by Andrei Tarkovsky and released in 1971.
32 Karen Blixen (2011) *Babette's Feast*. London: Penguin Books.
33 Hans Christian Andersen (1835/2008) 'The Princess and the Pea' in *Fairy Tales of Hans Christian Andersen*, retrieved from www.gutenberg.org/ebooks/27200.

34 Bruce Sterling (2011) 'The Future of Making' in Daniel Charny (ed.) *Power of Making: The Importance of Being Skilled.* London: V&A Publishing.

35 Alvin Toffler (1970) *Future Shock.* London: Random House. Toffler coined the term 'prosumers' when he predicted that the role of producers and consumers would begin to blur and merge.

36 Neil Gershenfeld (2011) 'The Making Revolution: In Conversation with Daniel Charny, 24 March 2011' in Charny (ed.) *Power of Making.*

37 Sterling, 'The Future of Making', p. 59.

38 Ibid., p. 61.

39 Ibid., p. 67.

40 Stitch 'n Bitch (2014) *Find a Knitting Group or Start Your Own,* retrieved from http://stitchnbitch. org.

41 3rd Revolution (2014) *3rd Revolution is a New Online Community for Crafters,* retrieved from www.about.3rdrevolution.com.

42 Sterling, 'The Future of Making', p. 68.

43 Ibid.

44 Sennett, *The Craftsman,* p. 20.

45 Martina Margetts (2011) 'Actions not Words' in Charny (ed.) *Power of Making,* p. 39.

46 Sennett, *The Craftsman.*

47 Thorstein Veblen (1918) *The Instinct of Workmanship and the State of the Industrial Arts.* New York: B.W. Huebsch.

48 Richard Sennett (2012) *Together: The Rituals, Pleasures and Politics of Cooperation.* London: Penguin Books, p. 19.

49 Ibid.

50 Ibid., p. 117.
51 Joke Brouwer and Sjoerd van Tuinen (2014) 'Preface', in Brouwer and van Tuinen (eds.) *Giving and Taking: Antidotes to a Culture of Greed.* Rotterdam: V2_Publishing, p. 5.
52 See Peter Sloterdijk 'What Does a Human Have That He Can Give Away?' in Brouwer and van Tuinen (eds.) *Giving and Taking*, pp. 10–11.
53 Sennett, *Together*, p. 50ff.
54 Ibid., p. 39.

6 Crises and consequences

1 The last few years have brought a number of high-profile publications critically examining income and wealth inequality, such as Branko Milanovic (2010) *The Haves and Have-nots: A Brief and Idiosyncratic History of Global Inequality.* New York: Basic Books; or Richard Wilkinson and Kate Pickett (2009) *The Spirit Level: Why Equality Is Better for Everyone.* London: Penguin Books. But none of these and similar books created a stir comparable to that of the English edition of Piketty's work: Thomas Piketty (2014) *Capital in the Twenty-First Century.* Cambridge, MA: Harvard University Press.
2 Jerzy Kociatkiewicz and Monika Kostera (2010), 'Experiencing the Shadow: Organizational Exclusion and Denial within Experience Economy', *Organization* 17/2: 257–82.
3 Arlie Russell Hochschild (2012) *The Outsourced Self: Intimate Life in Market Times.* New York: Metropolitan Books.
4 Ibid., p. 223.
5 Kurt Lewin, Ronald Lippit and Ralph K. White

(1939) 'Patterns of Aggressive Behavior in Experimentally Created Social Climates', *Journal of Social Psychology* 10: 271–301.

6 Karl E. Weick (1969) *The Social Psychology of Organizing.* Reading: Addison-Wesley.

7 Eileen Appelbaum and Rosemary Batt (1994) *The New American Workplace: Transforming Work Systems in the United States.* Ithaca: Cornell University Press.

8 Jan de Leede, André H. J. Nijhof and Olaf A. M. Fisscher (1999) 'The Myth of Self-Managing Teams: A Reflection on the Allocation of Responsibilities between Individuals, Teams and the Organisation', *Journal of Business Ethics* 21/2–3: 203–15.

9 Ulla Johansson (1998) *Om Ansvar. Ansvarsföreställningar och Deras Betydelse för den Organisatoriska Verkligheten.* Lund: Lund University Press.

10 Robert E. Kelley (1988) 'In Praise of Followers', *Harvard Business Review* 66: 142–8.

11 Barbara Czarniawska (1992) *Exploring Complex Organizations: A Cultural Perspective.* Newbury Park: Sage.

12 Simon Kelly, Marian Iszatt White, Dave Martin and Mark Rouncefield (2006) 'Leadership Refrains: Patterns of Leadership', *Leadership* 2/2: 181–201.

13 Lisa Ehrich and Fenwick English (2012) 'Leadership as Dance: A Consideration of the Applicability of the 'Mother' of All Arts as the Basis for Establishing Connoisseurship', *International Journal of Leadership in Education: Theory and Practice* 16/4: 1–28.

---

14 Alf Rehn (2001) *Electronic Potlatch: A Study Concerning New Technologies and Primitive Economic Behaviors*. Stockholm: KTH.

15 Marcel Mauss (1950/2002) *The Gift*. London: Routledge.

16 Dariusz Jemielniak (2014) *Common Knowledge? An Ethnography of Wikipedia*. Redwood City, CA: Stanford University Press.

17 ITU (2014) 'The World in 2014: ICT Facts and Figures', retrieved from: www.itu.int/en/ITU-D/Statistics/Documents/facts/ICTFactsFigures2014-e.pdf.

18 Arlie Russell Hochschild (2012) *The Outsourced Self: Intimate Life in Market Times*. New York: Metropolitan Books.

19 Ibid., pp. 7ff.

20 Robert Kuttner (2007) *Everything for Sale: The Virtues and Limits of Markets*. New York: Alfred A. Knopf.

21 Hochschild, *The Outsourced Self*, p. 124.

22 Arlie Russell Hochschild (1983) *The Managed Heart: Commercialization of Human Feeling*, Los Angeles: University of California Press.

23 Ibid., pp. 222–3.

24 Stockholm Resilience Centre (2014) *What is Resilience? An Introduction to Social-Ecological Research*, retrieved from www.stockholmresilience.su.se.

25 Irena Bauman (2014) 'Day after Tomorrow'. Presentation at 'We Need to Talk' international symposium organized by Sustainia, 7 April 2014, in Copenhagen to discuss communication strategy for the forthcoming Synthesis Report of the 5th

Assessment Report of the Intergovernmental Panel on Climate Change (IPCC) published 31 October 2014. The report contained harsh messages about the impact of climate change.

26 Jonathan Rowson (2013) *New Agenda for Climate Change*. London: RSA.

27 Sally Weintrobe (2014) 'Discussion on Papers by Chris Ripley and Rob Nixon, Talking about Climate Change in Culture of Uncare', in *Proceedings from the 103rd Annual Meeting of the American Psychoanalytic Association, University Forum on 'How Do We Think about Climate Change?'*, p. 2.

28 Ibid., p. 3.

29 Suggestion quoted from Stockholm Resilience Centre, *What is Resilience?*.

30 Weintrobe, 'Discussion', p. 4.

31 E.g. Manfred Kets de Vries (2003) *Essays on the Psychology of Leadership: Leaders, Fools, and Imposters*. New York: iUniverse; Richard Pech and Bret W. Slade (2007) 'Organisational Sociopaths: Rarely Challenged, Often Promoted. Why?' *Society and Business Review* 2/3: 254–69.

32 Zygmunt Bauman (1987) *Legislators and Interpreters*. Cambridge and Oxford: Polity.

33 Krzysztof Obłój, *Zarządzanie: Ujęcie Praktyczne*. Warsaw: PWE.

34 An imperative whose importance is increasingly realized even by mainstream managers: see, e.g., Krzysztof Obłój (2013) *The Passion and Discipline of Strategy*. London: Palgrave Macmillan.

35 Mihaela Kelemen (2003) *Managing Quality: Managerial and Critical Perspectives*. London: Sage Publications.

36 Adrian Wilkinson and Hugh Willmott (1995) *Making Quality Critical: New Perspectives on Organizational Change*. London: Routledge.

37 See, e.g., Andrzej K. Koźmiński's definition of management as 'a journey through chaos, the essence of which is dominance over variety and transformation of potential conflict into cooperation', from Koźmiński (2002) 'Zarządzanie' in Koźmiński and Włodzimierz Piotrowski (eds.) *Zarządzanie: Teoria i Praktyka* (*Management: Theory and Practice*). Warsaw: PWN (pp. 45–83), pp. 56–7.

38 On the necessity of inclusion of a radical diversity of perspectives in striving towards deep organizational quality, see, e.g., Martyna Śliwa (2006) 'Service Quality Measurement: A Study of Appointments Systems in General Practice Surgeries'. Doctoral thesis, Newcastle: Newcastle Business School; and Monika Kostera and Martyna Śliwa (2013) *Zarządzanie w XXI Wieku: Jakość, Twórczość, Kultura* (*Management in the 21st Century: Quality, Creativity, Culture*). Warsaw: Wolters Kluwer.

39 William Ross Ashby (1956) *An Introduction to Cybernetics*. London: Chapman & Hall.

40 Obłój *The Passion and Discipline of Strategy*.

Coda

1 Simon Kelly (2014) 'Horses for Courses: Exploring the Limits of Leadership Development through Equine-assisted Learning', *Journal of Management Education* 38/2: 216–33.

2 Heather Höpfl (2000) 'Sacred Heart: A Comment on the Heart of Management', *Culture and Organization* 14/3: 225–40.

3 Joni Mitchell (1969) *Woodstock*. MCA, produced by Ian Matthews.
4 Lina D. (2014) '21 Photos of Nature Winning the Battle against Civilization', *BoredPanda*, retrieved from www.boredpanda.com/nature-reclaiming-civilization.
5 See, e.g., David Graeber (2013) *The Democracy Project: A History, a Crisis, a Movement*. New York: Spiegel & Grau, pp. 293–4.
6 Emmanuel Lévinas (1999) *Alterity and Transcendence*. London: The Athlone Press.